Top 10 Corsica Highlights

The Top 10 of Everything

CONTENTS

Corsica
Area by Area

Streetsmart

The information in this DK Eyewitness Top 10 Travel Guide is checked regularly. Every effort has been made to ensure that this book is as up-to-date as possible at the time of going to press. Some details, however, such as telephone numbers, opening hours, prices, gallery hanging arrangements and travel information, are liable to change. The publishers cannot accept responsibility for any consequences arising from the use of this book, nor for any material on third party websites, and cannot guarantee that any website address in this book will be a suitable source of travel information. We value the views and suggestions of our readers very highly. Please write to: Publisher, DK Eyewitness Travel Guides, Dorling Kindersley, 80 Strand, London WC2R 0RL,UK, or email travelguides@dk.com

Welcome to
Corsica

Napoleon said he could recognize his native island just by the fragrance of the maquis. Corsica is an enigmatic island, and the "Island of Beauty", as the French call it, lives up to its name. It has towering mountains, lush forests, timeless villages, stylish resorts and pristine beaches. With Eyewitness Top 10 Corsica, it's yours to explore.

The island's chic seaside resorts – **Calvi**, **St-Florent**, **Porto-Vecchio**, **Propriano** and lively capital **Ajaccio** – are surrounded by some of the Mediterranean's most beautiful beaches. On the west coast, there's the astonishing **Golfe de Porto**, framed on either end by the bizarre porphyry rock formations of the **Calanche de Piana** and the savage pink cliffs of **Scandola**. The long, narrow peninsula of **Cap Corse** is lined with vertiginous villages, vineyards and seascapes.

Inland, Corsica's untamed beauty is one of its greatest draws. The **Parc Naturel Régional de Corse** protects 40 per cent of the island's wilderness, encompassing one of the most demanding high-altitude trails in the world, the **GR20**. Yet along with this wild terrain, evidence of Corsica's unique history abounds: the 5,000-year-old standing stones of **Filitosa**, medieval Pisan churches and the austerely beautiful old mountain capital **Corte** are wonderfully evocative. Traces of more recent history can be found in **Ajaccio**, home to one of France's finest provincial museums and a vast range of Napoleonic artifacts.

Whether you're visiting for a weekend or a week, our Top 10 guide brings together the best of everything Corsica has to offer, from historic **Bonifacio** to bustling **Bastia**. The guide has useful tips throughout, from seeking out what's free to avoiding the crowds, plus six easy-to-follow itineraries, designed to tie together a clutch of sights in a short space of time. Add inspiring photography and detailed maps, and you've got the essential pocket-sized travel companion. **Enjoy the book, and enjoy Corsica.**

Clockwise from top: **Plage de Rondinara**; Porto village, Les Calanches; Rue Notre Dame, Bastia; Sant'Antonino church; cemetery in Propriano; Quai Comparetti, Bonifacio; relief showing a grape harvest at San Michele de Murato, Nebbio

Exploring Corsica

Although sights may not look far apart on a map of the island, Corsica's mountainous roads make it essential to plan your exploration wisely. On the plus side, the scenery is so staggeringly beautiful that the journey is part of the pleasure. Here are a few ideas to help maximize your time.

The fishing harbour at Ajaccio is lined with bars and restaurants.

Two Days in Ajaccio

Day ❶
MORNING
Take the walking tour around town (*see p79*), including a couple of hours in the Musée des Beaux Arts in the **Palais Fesch** (*see pp14–15; closed Tue*).
AFTERNOON
Travel by boat or bus across to **Porticcio** (*see p80*) for lunch, and then spend a lazy afternoon at the beautiful **plage de Verghia** (*see p77*).

Day ❷
MORNING
Watch fishermen bringing in the day's catch at the fishing harbour, before buying picnic supplies at the open-air food market. Stop by Ajaccio's historic cemetery on the way to **Les Millelli** (*see p13*), the Bonapartes' country house, for a picnic.
AFTERNOON
Visit the tortoises at **A Cupulatta** (*see p80*), and then take a cruise out to the **Îles Sanguinaires** (*see p12*) to see the famous red sunset.

Seven Days in Corsica

Day ❶
From Ajaccio, head south to the beach-fringed **Golfe de Valinco** (*see pp16–17*). Visit Filitosa, Corsica's most important megalithic site, before having lunch and a swim at the nearby Porto-Pollo. Afterwards, take a drive up to the austere granite town of **Sartène** (*see p18*) and visit the Musée Départemental de Préhistoire de Corse et d'Archéologie.

Day ❷
Pick up picnic supplies and, in the cool of the morning, explore the wild landscapes and megaliths of **Le Sartenais** (*see pp18–19*) before hitting the stunning **plage de Roccapina** (*see p50*). In the afternoon, head over to **Bonifacio** (*see pp20–21*) and take a boat trip (*see p48*) under the cliffs. Afterwards, visit the *haute ville* (old town), which is extremely evocative (and much less crowded) after dark.

Day ❸
Start off the day at the **plage de Palombaggia** (*see p87*), then peruse the chic boutiques of **Porto-Vecchio** (*see p86*). Afterwards, travel to the

Golfe de Valinco is known for its stunning blue waters and forest-covered hillsides.

The Aiguilles de Bavella are visible for miles around.

Key
— Two-day itinerary
— Seven-day itinerary

0 km   20
0 miles   20

(map labels) Col de Teghime · Désert des Agriate · L'Île-Rousse · St-Florent · Bastia · Calvi · Balagne · Corniche · Corte · Calanche de Piana · Porto · Evisa · Vallée de la Restonica · Piana · Forêt d'Aïtone · Vizzavone · Aléria · A Cupulatta · Ajaccio · Porticcio · Îles Sanguinaires · BOAT · Plage de Verghia · Filitosa · Aiguilles de Bavella · Porto-Pollo · Golfe de Valinco · Sartène · Porto-Vecchio · Le Sartenais · Plage de Palombaggia · Plage de Roccapina · Bonifacio

Aiguilles de Bavella (Bavella needles) *(see p87)* for lunch with a view over the majestic peaks. Journey to the east coast to ancient Greek and Roman **Aléria** *(see p94)*; from here it's 90 minutes to **Bastia** *(pp22–3)*. Arrive just in time for dinner by the bijou fishing port.

Day ❹
Spend the morning in Bastia's Place du Marché, and explore the city's lively streets and Baroque churches. Visit the **Musée de Bastia** *(see p22; closed Mon)* in the Citadelle. Make the spectacular drive inland over the Col de Teghime to pretty **St-Florent** *(see pp28–9)*.

Day ❺
Drive across the Désert des Agriate *(see p28)* to **L'Île Rousse** *(see p100)*. Have a look around, then take a scenic tour of the **Balagne** *(see p100)* before ending up at **Calvi** *(see pp30–31)*. Visit Calvi's Genoese Citadelle, and finish the day sipping an apéritif on swanky Quai Landry.

Day ❻
Get an early start to make the scenic drive down the **Corniche** *(see p35)* to **Porto** *(see p34)*. Carry on to the extraordinary red **Calanche de Piana** *(see p49)* for lunch. Head for the mountains, stopping at **Evisa** *(see p81)* for a hike in the **Forêt d'Aïtone** *(see p48)*. End the day at **Corte** *(see p32)*.

Day ❼
Visit the **Musée de la Corse** *(see p33)* and take a short excursion up the enchanting **Vallée de la Restonica** *(see p93)*. After lunch, head back to Ajaccio. If you have time, stop for a forest walk at **Vizzavona** *(see p95)*.

Top 10 Corsica Highlights

The dramatic cliff face at Bonifacio

🔟 Corsica Highlights

Corsica encapsulates the best the Mediterranean has to offer. Protected by environmental laws, its coastline has escaped the kind of development seen in the Rivieras, while the forests, gorges and crumbling villages inland have altered little in centuries. The island also preserves a wealth of historic monuments, from Bronze Age menhirs to Genoese citadels.

Ajaccio ①
Beneath the Mediterranean chic of its high-rise outskirts, the capital of Corsica has retained a strong historic accent, underlined by the Palais Fesch, with its priceless artworks (see pp12–15).

② Golfe de Valinco
Wild hillsides sweep from the shores of the Golfe de Valinco, where the white-sand shoreline is dotted with small resorts and, just inland, extraordinary prehistoric sites (see pp16–17).

Le Sartenais ③
Head here if you are searching for wilderness. Standing stones are strewn over a landscape of pristine Mediterranean scrub, edged by a succession of remote beaches (see pp18–19).

⑤ Bastia
Facing Tuscany across the Tyrrhenian Sea, Bastia has a more chaotic, Italian feel than southern rival Ajaccio, most pervasive in the picturesque Vieux Port (see pp22–3).

④ Bonifacio
The striated chalk cliffs of Bonifacio are an iconic sight. A perfectly preserved Genoese *haute ville* (upper town) perches on the cliffs above the translucent turquoise water (see pp20–21).

6 Cap Corse
Lovely views of the distant Tuscan Islands lend this peninsula, north of Bastia, a special atmosphere – best savoured with the local muscat wine *(see pp26–7)*.

7 St-Florent and the Nebbio
This pretty port is a world away from the bustle of Bastia. Travel across its gulf to swim in some dazzlingly turquoise coves *(see pp28–9)*.

8 Calvi
Calvi's weathered Genoese Citadelle stands over a sweep of white sand and sparkling sea water *(see pp30–31)*.

9 Corte and its Hinterland
The mountain town of Corte occupies a grandiose setting. Its crow's-nest Citadelle is dwarfed by vast escarpments and snowy peaks *(see pp32–3)*.

10 Golfe de Porto
Admire the scenery of the northwest, where red cliffs plunge into a deep-blue gulf. Take a boat to the Calanche rock formations *(see pp34–5)*.

TOP 10 ⭐ Ajaccio

With a backdrop of wild, granite mountains and lapis-blue sea, Ajaccio ranks among the most splendidly sited capitals in the Mediterranean. Travellers from Edward Lear to Guy de Maupassant were enthralled by its setting, and the imperial city remains an essential stop for visitors – not least because of its association with Napoleon, who was born and raised here. The Bonapartes' former residence lies in the heart of a grid of narrow, weather-worn alleys, where you can sip pastis at a pavement café while the locals take their afternoon *passeghiata* (walk), or enjoy fresh seafood straight off the boats.

2 Îles Sanguinaires

One of the short stories in Alphonse Daudet's famous *Lettres de mon Moulin*, was inspired by a visit to this archipelago of islets, tapering into the sea **(left)**.

1 Lazaret Ollandini

Halfway along the coastal road to the airport, this former quarantine station is now a performance venue. It hosts operas and concerts, and contains the Marc Petit Museum, which features art exhibitions.

3 Fishing Harbour

Ajaccio's tiny fishing quay **(right)**, just south of the marina, is a great place to visit early in the morning, when the night's catch is being landed against a backdrop of palms, yachts and giant ferries.

NAPOLEON AND CORSICA

Born in Ajaccio, Napoleon spent his formative years in Paris, becoming a passionate advocate of the French Revolution, which did little to endear him to Pascal Paoli's nationalist regime back home. Having been chased into exile by Paoli's supporters, Napoleon shunned his homeland for good, returning only once, briefly, while en route to France after his Egyptian campaign.

4 Ajaccio Cathedral

A brooding Delacroix painting of the Virgin holding the Sacred Heart sets a sombre tone for visits to this late Baroque cathedral **(above)**, where Napoleon was baptized.

5 Open-Air Food Market

Each weekday during the tourist season, producers from across the island descend on place Foch, in front of the Town Hall, to sell honey, herbs and artisanal sausages.

Map of Ajaccio

Maison Bonaparte ⑨

The Bonapartes lived here until Paolist rebels drove them into exile in 1793. Don't miss the sofa on which Napoleon **(right)** was born.

⑩ Palais Fesch

This museum boasts a fine collection of Renaissance and Baroque art. Highlights include *Leda and the Swan*, a 16th-century painting by Paolo Veronese.

⑥ Citadelle

Originally built by the Genoese, the hexagonal citadel juts into the bay next to St-François beach. The fortress played a key role in Corsican history, jailing resistance fighters in World War II.

⑦ Les Millelli

Nestled in an olive grove, Les Millelli was the Bonapartes' country retreat. Napoleon stayed here during his last visit to Ajaccio in 1799. The grounds make for an excellent picnic spot.

⑧ Salon Napoléonien

Napoleon's death mask is among the quirky memorabilia on show at this small museum **(below)** inside the Hôtel de Ville on place Foch.

NEED TO KNOW

Tourist Office: **MAP H3**; 3 Blvd du Roi Jérome; 04955 15303; www.ajaccio-tourisme.com

Lazaret Ollandini: **MAP H3**; Quartier Aspretto; 04951 08515; Marc Petit Museum: check website for opening hours; www.lelazaret-ollandini.com

Salon Napoléonien: **MAP P2**; Place Foch; 04955 15253; open 9–11:45am & 2–4:45pm (to 5:45pm mid-Jun–mid-Sep); closed summer: Mon am; winter: Sat & Sun

Maison Bonaparte: **MAP P3**; Rue St Charles; 04952 14389; open Apr–Sep: 10am–12:30pm & 1:15–5:30pm; Oct–Mar: 10:30am–12:30pm & 1:15–4:30pm; closed Mon, 25 Dec, 1 Jan; adm; www.musees-nationaux-malmaison.fr

Palais Fesch: **MAP P1**; 50–52 Rue Cardinal Fesch; 04952 62626; open May–Oct: 9:15am–6pm; Jul & Aug: noon–8pm Fri; Nov–Apr: 9am–5pm; closed first 2 wks in Jan; adm €8; www.musee-fesch.com

■ The Ajaccio Tourist Office offers tours from April to September (by request in other months).

■ Grand Café Napoléon is a great place for a Corsican coffee *(see p83)*.

Palais Fesch – Musée des Beaux Arts

Botticelli's _Virgin and Child_

1 Botticelli's Virgin and Child with an Angel

Virgin and Child with an Angel is one of the finest in a series of devotional pictures painted by Sandro Botticelli (1445–1510), a great master of the early Renaissance. The Virgin's open display of affection makes the painting one of the loveliest works in the museum.

2 Gaulli's Joseph Recites a Dream to His Brothers

Also known as Il Baciccio, Giovanni Battista Gaulli (1639–1709) was Bernini's protégé and a veteran of the Baroque style. This painting is presented in the museum's large gallery next to its companion piece _Joseph Recognised by His Brothers_. The subject of these pieces is taken from the Old Testament and relates to two episodes in the life of Joseph.

3 Titian's Portrait of a Man with a Glove

The jewel in the crown of the Palais Fesch collection is this exquisite portrait by legendary Venetian artist Titian (c.1488–1576). Here, he limits the colours he uses and darkens the background, focusing in on the hands and expression of the sitter to create a sense of psychological presence.

4 Tommaso's Mystical Marriage of St Catherine

The figure kneeling in the foreground here is St Catherine of Alexander, who is said to have had a vision in which Christ took her as his spiritual bride in the presence of the Virgin Mary. It is a fine example of early Renaissance art by Niccolò di Tommaso (c.1346–76).

5 Bernini's Portrait of David

One of the masters of the Italian Baroque, Gianlorenzo Bernini (1598–1680) enjoyed an illustrious career as a sculptor and architect. He was also an exceptional portrait painter, and sometimes worked with his 'entourage', as in this brooding, psychologically intense work.

6 Veronese's Leda and the Swan

This erotic painting by Paolo Veronese (1528–88) depicts a scene from Greek mythology in which Zeus seduces Leda (the mother of Helen of Troy). It is prized for its titillating subject matter, a recurrent motif in Renaissance paintings.

7 Gérard's Napoleon in Coronation Robes

François Gérard (1770–1837) painted all the leading figures of the Napoleonic period in France, especially the recently crowned emperor, who is shown here in full regalia. The work is the highlight of the museum's Napoleonic collection.

8 Recco's Still Life with Fish and Lobster

Few visitors pass this still life by Neapolitan artist Giuseppe Recco (1634–95) without pausing in awe at its photo-realisitic quality.

9 Tura's Virgin Mary and Child with St Jerome and a Holy Martyr

This 15th-century painting by the Italian painter Cosmè Tura of Ferrara (c.1433–95) was bequeathed by Cardinal Fesch to the city of Ajaccio in 1839.

10 Solimena's The Departure of Rebecca

Francesco Solimena (1657–1747) was one of the most prolific and successful figures of the Baroque period, and his strength lay in the creation of dramatic biblical scenes. This painting depicts Rebecca leaving for her marriage to Isaac, the son of Abraham.

Solimena's *The Departure of Rebecca*

A CARDINAL'S COLLECTION

Cardinal Joseph Fesch, Napoleon's step-uncle, owned a large personal fortune and had a great eye for a bargain, at a time when Europe's art markets were awash with loot plundered by the French armies. The result was the largest private collection of paintings and classical sculpture in the world – a total of 16,000 pieces spanning five centuries. While most of the Cardinal's estate was left to Napoleon's family after his death in 1839, he bequeathed 1,500 pieces to Ajaccio. However, Fesch's principal heir, Napoleon's elder brother, contested this bequest, and the family sold off the bulk of the estate before the legal case was resolved. Masterpieces from the collection can now be seen in many of the national galleries in Europe. Early Renaissance art of the "Quattrocento" period was, on the other hand, undervalued at the time, so that today's Fesch collection includes an array of 15th- and early 16th-century Italian masterpieces.

TOP 10 EVENTS IN THE LIFE OF JOSEPH FESCH

1 Born in Ajaccio in 1763

2 Left for Toulon with the Bonapartes in 1793

3 Became Archbishop of Lyon in 1802

4 Appointed ambassador to Rome by Napoleon in 1803 until 1806

5 Received Légion d'Honneur in 1804

6 Napoleon annexed Papal States in 1809, causing friction with the Cardinal

7 Fesch fell out with Napoleon after he detained the Pope in 1812

8 Returned to Lyon from Rome in 1815

9 Retired to Rome after Napoleon's abdication in 1815

10 Died in Rome in 1839

Visiting Palais Fesch is a must for art lovers, especially fans of the Renaissance period.

TOP 10 ⭐ Golfe de Valinco

The most southerly of the four great gulfs indenting Corsica's west coast, Valinco presents an arresting spectacle when seen from the high ridges enfolding it. Its vivid blue waters cleave into the heart of the Alta Rocca region, where orange-roofed settlements cling to hillsides smothered in holm-oak forest and impenetrable maquis. People come here to laze on the string of sandy beaches, although some stupendous views are to be had from the ancient granite perched villages inland, which were the refuge of local inhabitants during the repeated pirate raids in the 15th and 16th centuries.

1 Propriano
A sleepy village out of season **(above)**, Propriano is a bustling resort and ferry port in the summer, when visitors throng the stylish waterfront café terraces lining the town's marina.

4 Fozzano
The real-life heroine of Prosper Mérimée's vendetta novel *Colomba* was from this village **(right)**. The granite tower-houses recall the conflicts that beset the region in the 1800s.

2 Filitosa
Corsica's famed prehistoric site is renowned for its collection of carved standing stones. Their eerily defiant features **(left)** were chiselled from granite 5,000 years ago.

3 Porto-Pollo
This fishing village serves as the region's scuba-diving hub, as well as a base for trips to hidden beaches.

5 Gulf Cruises
Excursion boats leave daily from Propriano Marina in the summer, calling at several coves, snorkelling hot spots and photogenic rock formations only reachable by sea. Some outfits offer romantic sunset cruises.

⑥ Campomoro

Spread behind a shell-shaped bay that is overlooked by a watchtower **(above)**, Campomoro is a quiet and secluded spot.

⑧ Plage de Cupabia

Valinco's loveliest beach is the place to sidestep the summer crowds. Hidden over the hill from Porto-Pollo, it lies beyond the range of day-tripping Ajaccians, in a gloriously wild setting.

⑨ Col de Siu

An unforgettable drive inland from Propriano on the little-used D557 culminates in this lonely pass, visited by more goats than people. Scramble over the rocks for magnificent views of the gulf.

Map of Golfe de Valinco

⑦ Ste-Lucie de Tallano

Bucolic olive and almond groves surround this picturesque Alta Rocca village *(see p44)*. Taste cold-pressed oil in a mill outlet, or watch *pétanque* players on a plane-shaded square.

⑩ Bains de Caldanes

One of Valinco's quirkier attractions is this tiny hot spring, situated just 6 km (4 miles) from Ste-Lucie de Tallano. Its waters bubble at an invigorating 40°C (104°F).

VENDETTA IN CORSICA

Corsica is infamous for the blood feuds that wracked the island in past centuries. Valinco was the worst-affected region. The forbidding appearance of many old houses, with fortified rooftops and no ground-floor doorways, gives a sense of how pervasive the violence was. Fozzano is a prime example – its feud was the backdrop to Prosper Mérimée's 19th-century blockbuster *Colomba*.

NEED TO KNOW

Tourist Office: **MAP H5**; Quai St-Erasme, Propriano; 04957 60149; www.lacorsedesorigines.com

Filitosa: **MAP J4**; 10 km (6 miles) inland from Porto-Pollo on the D157; 04957 40091; open Apr–Oct: 9am–sunset; adm €7; www.filitosa.fr

Gulf Cruises: Promenades en mer à Propriano; port de Plaisance; 06125 49928; mid-May–mid-Oct; €38 (sunrise cruise), €34 (sunset cruise)

Bains de Caldanes: **MAP K5**; D148 route de Granace, Ste-Lucie de Tallano; 04957 35026; Open 9am–8pm daily (Jul & Aug: to 11:30pm); adm €5

■ Festivities such as music, street performances and late-night shopping take place in Sartène *(see p18)* on Thursday nights in summer.

■ A Madunnina on the road between Propriano and Sartène serves wood-fired pizzas.

TOP 10 ⭐ Le Sartenais

Coastal wilderness is a rarity in the Mediterranean these days, especially where there are sublime beaches. However, the southwest of Corsica has remained astonishingly untrammelled. Forced out by pirates and the collapse of the wine industry, its inhabitants left the maquis a century or so ago to the ghosts of their prehistoric ancestors, whose tombs and standing stones are still strewn all over the countryside. Roads will only take you so far in this region: you will need solid shoes and lots of bottled water for the full experience.

1 A Casa di Roccapina

This museum covers the history and legends of Roccapina's bizarre *tafoni* rocks and manmade shelters (*oriu*), and offers an audio-guided walk.

A view across Le Sartenais

NEED TO KNOW

MAP J6 ■ Tourist Office: 14 cours Soeur Amélie; 04957 71540; www.lacorsedesorigines.com

A Casa di Roccapina: RN196; 04957 15630; open mid-Apr–mid-Oct: daily; mid-Oct–mid-Apr: Tue–Sat; closed 20 Dec– 4 Jan; adm €2

Musée Départemental de Préhistoire Corse et d'Archéologie: Blvd Jacques Nicolaï, Sartène; 04957 70109; open Jun–Sep: 10am–6pm daily; Oct–May: 10am– 5pm Mon–Fri; closed public hols; adm €4

Domaine Saparale: D50 Vallée de l'Ortolo, Saparale Sartène; 04957 71552; www.saparale.com; visits by appt

Site Archéologique de Cauria: RD48A; 04952 91300

■ For lunch, pop in at the roadside Bergerie d'Acciola (*see p89*).

2 Musée Départemental de Préhistoire Corse et d'Archéologie

The finest collection of prehistoric artifacts on the island, some dating back to the early Neolithic age **(left)**, are housed at this museum. It is an ideal primer for tours of this region's standing-stone sites.

3 Sartène

"The most Corsican of Corsican towns" is how Merimée described Sartène **(right)** in the 19th century. Its medieval buildings retain a dark undertone, echoed in the ancient Easter U Catenacciu parade (*see p70*).

**Map of
Le Sartenais**

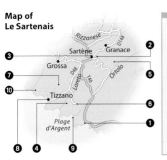

U CATENACCIU

Nothing conveys the aura of secrecy surrounding Corsican culture like the Easter processions of hooded penitents. Among these haunting parades, U Catenacciu, held on Good Friday in Sartène, is the oldest and most uncanny. The identity of the red-robed "Grand Pénitent" is kept a secret, as the role perennially appeals to prominent mafiosi and fugitives from justice.

6 Site Archéologique de Cauria

This Neolithic archaeological site holds the Stantari and Rinaghju alignments, with 22 phallic menhirs amid the maquis south of Sartène.

7 Alignement de Palaggiu

This is Corsica's largest collection of standing-stones, where 250 statue-menhirs cluster in a clearing **(right)**.

8 Tizzano and Cala di l'Avena

Huddled around an inlet hemmed in by boulder-studded hills, Tizzano is among the island's most remote fishing villages. The nearby Cala di l'Avena beach is a marvel.

10 Sentier des Douaniers

The former Genoese custom-officers' path is now a world-class coast walk. It takes you along the rugged Sartenais shoreline via a non-stop parade of wild beaches, turquoise coves and the lonely Senetosa watchtower.

4 Dolmen de Fontanaccia

Known to locals as "The Devil's Forge", this late-megalithic burial chamber comprises six huge boulders topped by a slab. It is best viewed in the warm light of the setting sun.

5 Vallée de l'Ortolo

Overlooked by grey-granite cliffs, this empty valley just south of Sartène encapsulates the region's austere beauty. Visit the Domaine Saparale vineyard *(see p69)* to savour the valley's vintage wines.

9 Plage d'Erbaju

Clamber to the top of the headland overlooking Roccapina's white sandy beach, crowned with a crumbling watch-tower **(below)** and rock outcrop resembling a recumbent lion, to pick up the path to deserted Erbaju beach.

TOP 10 ⭐ Bonifacio

Bonifacio is Corsica's foremost visitor attraction and, despite all the commotion in high season, it more than merits the distinction. Spread over the top of a long, narrow promontory that is encircled on three sides by sheer chalk escarpments, the medieval Genoese *haute ville* (upper town) looks on one side across the straits to Sardinia and on the other over its secluded harbour, a port Homer mentions in *The Odyssey*. Aside from wandering around the ancient alleyways of the Citadelle, the other unmissable activity here is taking a boat trip for a view of the fabled white cliffs from water level.

① Quai Comparetti
Quai Comparetti's café-restaurants are the perfect place to soak up the atmosphere of Bonifacio's marina, with its constant traffic of excursion boats and millionaires' yachts.

② Chapelle Roch
This tiny shrine at the head of Montée Rastello is where Bonifacio's last plague victim died in the epidemic of 1518. Steps lead down to some superb snorkelling sites.

③ Escalier du Roi d'Aragon
Get hands-on experience of Bonifacio's chalk cliffs with a hike down this flight of 187 steps, hewn from rock in medieval times, to reach a hidden freshwater well.

The dramatic cliffs of Bonifacio

Map of Bonifacio

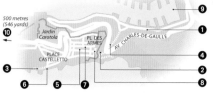

500 metres
(546 yards)
Jardin Carotola
PL DES ARMES
PLACE CASTELLETTO
AV CHARLES-DE-GAULLE

④ Montée Rastello
This flight of stone steps leads from the port to a raised balcony below the entrance to the Citadelle, for a stunning view of the "Grain de Sable" rock stack and cliffs.

7 Rue du Palais de Garde

Multi-storeyed tenements with estucheon-embellished doorways flank this medieval street **(left)**. Residents still use winches to lift supplies to upper floors.

5 Ste-Marie-Majeure

Relics of the True Cross, said to have been donated by Emperor Constantine's mother St Helena, after she was saved from a shipwreck in the straits, number among the treasures enshrined in Bonifacio's historic church **(below)**.

THE WRECK OF THE SÉMILLANTE

They might look gorgeous on a sunny day, but the Straits of Bonifacio rank among the most fickle waterways in the world, with notoriously unpredictable currents and volatile weather. In 1885, the troop carrier *Sémillante* ran aground off the Îles Lavezzi while en route to the Crimea. An obelisk on the westernmost islet commemorates the tragedy, in which 773 people lost their lives.

9 Boat Trips

Hop on a boat to take a close-up look at Bonifacio's resplendent white cliffs and *haute ville*. Some trips also take in the exquisite Îles Lavezzi.

6 Beaches Around Bonifacio

The chalky soils of the Bonifacio area helped create some of the Mediterranean's whitest, softest sand, especially at Sperone, Pianterella and Rondinara.

8 Porte de Gênes

In Genoese times, this turreted gateway, with its impressive drawbridge, was the only entrance to the Citadelle. Beyond it are breathtaking sea views from the terrace of the Jardins des Vestiges.

10 Cimetière des Marins

At the far western tip of the promontory lies a walled cemetery **(above)** containing the beautifully decorated tombs of deceased Bonifacians.

NEED TO KNOW

MAP K7 ■ Tourist Office: 2 Rue Fred Scamaroni, Quartier Pisan (additional locations open in summer & spring); 04957 31188; www.bonifacio.fr

Escalier du Roi d'Aragon: Haute Ville, Bonifacio; 04957 31188; open Apr–Sep: 9am–7:30pm (Jul & Aug: to 10:30pm); Oct: 10am–4:30pm; adm €2.50

Boat trips from Bonifacio Marina, Promenades en

Mer de Bonifacio, Quai Noël Beretti, Port de Bonifacio: 04951 09750; Sea Caves €17.40, Îles Lavezzi €35 (bring water, picnic, sun-block and swimwear)

■ Except in high season, the ticket prices quoted by touts for the boat trips in the marina will always drop if you haggle.

■ For a money-saving snack, try the Spar Supermarket just east of the Quai Comparetti.

TOP 10 ⭐ Bastia

Bastia is Corsica's commercial capital, with a more upbeat, big-city feel than Ajaccio. Since Genoese times, its nucleus has been a picturesque quarter of ramshackle old tenements, with buttressed walls and cobbled alleyways radiating from the harbour. The twin bell towers of the St-Jean-Baptiste church are the town's emblematic landmark. Behind the Vieux Port, an amphitheatre of high-rise suburbs look out to sea. The constant to-and-fro of ferries reminds you that Italy is just across the water, and its influence over Bastia's culture is ubiquitous.

1 Musée de Bastia

The Citadelle's fully renovated Governors' Palace holds a museum charting Bastia's evolution as a trade and artistic centre. Its collection includes part of Cardinal Fesch's hoard of Renaissance art.

3 Place St-Nicolas

Open to the sea on one side, Place St-Nicolas is where Bastiais come to wine, dine, stroll and play *pétanque* under the plane trees. A weekly flea market (open 6am–1pm) draws crowds on Sunday mornings.

2 Oratoire de l'Immaculée Conception

This Baroque chapel (1611) has an ornate interior **(above)**. Behind the altar is a painting of the Immaculate Conception by Bartolomé Esteban Murillo.

4 Place du Marché

This fresh-produce market is a source of local delicacies, as well as the perfect spot to people-watch over a leisurely coffee.

NEED TO KNOW

MAP F3 ■ Tourist Office: north end of Place St-Nicolas; 04955 42040; www.bastia-tourisme.com

Musée de Bastia: **MAP P6**; Place du Donjon, Citadelle; 04953 10912; open May–Sep: 10am–6:30pm Tue–Sun (Jul & Aug: daily); Oct–Apr: 9am–noon & 2–5pm Tue–Sat; adm €5, €1 for garden visit, (Nov–Apr free); www.musee-bastia.com

Place du Marché: **MAP P5**; open 7am–1pm Sat & Sun

La Canonica: **MAP F3;** Rte de la Canonica, Lucciana; open Jul & Aug: 9am–noon & 3–7pm daily, Pentecost Mon

DIAN'Arte Museum: **MAP P5**; 5992 Lido de la Marana, Borgo; 04953 61508; open 2–6pm Mon–Fri, Jul & Aug: 2–7pm daily; www.gabriel-diana.com

■ Art-house cinema Le Studio (www.studiocinema.fr) shows films in English.

■ Sample the delights of Raugi Glacier & Pizzeria (2 Rue du Chanoine Colombani; 04953 12231).

⑤ Vieux Port

Head to Bastia's old harbour **(below)** at sunset, when the cafés around it cast reflections in the limpid water. The tip of the harbour jetty provides the best viewpoint.

⑧ DIAN' Arte Museum

This museum is dedicated to artist and sculptor Gabriel Diana (b. 1942), who specializes in bronze figures inspired by the Etruscan sculptures of his native Tuscany **(left)**.

BASTIA IN WORLD WAR II

Bastia witnessed the most intense battle fought on Corsican soil during World War II, when Kesselring's army fled through the city back to the Italian mainland. Ironically, the worst casualties were sustained the day after the Nazi evacuation. Due to a mix-up in the Allied command, a squadron of American B-52 bombers destroyed the Vieux Port just as its inhabitants were out celebrating in their newly liberated streets.

Map of Bastia

AV MARÉCHAL SEBASTIANI

③
⑩
②
④
⑤
⑨ MONTÉE FILIPPINA ①
⑥
500 metres
(546 yards)

10 km
(6.2 miles) ⑧ ✈/⛴ 22 km (13.6 miles)

⑥ Cathédrale Ste-Marie and Oratoire Ste-Croix

This pair of majestic 15th-century rococo churches in Bastia's Citadelle hold miracle-working icons: the former a silver Virgin, the latter a blackened oak crucifix – "Christ des Miracles", which was fished out of the sea in 1428.

⑨ Scala Santa, Oratoire de Monserato

Bastia's most off-beat religious monument is a replica of the Holy Steps of St John Lateran's Basilica in Rome, which pilgrims ascend on their knees. Reach it from the Citadelle via the stepped Chemin des Fillipines.

⑩ Boulevard Paoli

Bastia's principal street is a grand thoroughfare, lined with impressive Napoleonic-era apartments and ritzy shops. The crowds usually begin to lessen after lunchtime.

La Canonica ⑦

Dating back to 1119, the stately La Canonica **(right)** is the finest of the 300 or so churches built by the Pisans across Corsica in the 12th century (see p42).

🔟 ⭐ Cap Corse

Before the construction in the 19th century of the corniche that circles Cap Corse, the long, finger-like promontory running north from Bastia was practically inaccessible except via sea. To a large extent, Cap Corse still feels like a separate island. Wine was its raison d'être under the Genoese, but production collapsed after the phylloxera epidemic of the early 1900s. However, the famous orange-blossom-scented muscat is still produced by a handful of growers, whose terraces cling to steep, fire-blackened slopes.

1 Macinaggio
Located on the northeastern tip of Cap Corse, Macinaggio and its marina have a remote feel. To get much further north, you must go on foot or jump on a boat.

2 Tour de Sénèque
The Roman philosopher Seneca, exiled to a tower above the village of Luri (below), found the views from his prison over the northern cape "desolate", but they are well worth the half-hour hike.

3 Tollare
A ribbon of tiny schist cottages clinging to the wave-lashed edge of Cap Corse, Tollare is the kind of place that makes you marvel at the resilience of its former inhabitants.

4 Nonza
Sweeping views across the Gulf of St-Florent extend from Nonza, a village atop a rock pinnacle, whose surrounding cliffs plunge to a beach (above).

5 Conservatoire du Cap Corse de Canari
In the cellars of the former convent of St François, Canari has set up two permanent exhibitions. One is dedicated to traditional costumes, and the other to historic photographs taken on Cap Corse by 120 local families.

Map of Cap Corse

6 The Corniche
The corniche winds around the entire cape. The section just north of Bastia has the best views, owing to its proximity to the Tuscan archipelago.

Previous pages Îles Sanguinaires

7 Erbalunga

A Genoese watchtower stands guard over Erbalunga's harbour – the prettiest port on the cape's eastern shore **(below)**. Affluent Bastiais drive up here to dine at the Michelin-starred Le Pirate restaurant *(see p103)*.

LES MAISONS D'AMÉRICAINS

Many Cap Corsicans took to the colonies of South and Central America to seek their fortune in the early 1800s. Having grown rich on gold prospecting or coffee planting, they returned to end their days in grand mansions that echoed the source of their owners' wealth. Known locally as "les maisons d'Américains", the villas lend an exotic flavour to the cape.

10 Site Naturelle de la Capandula

A trio of idyllic beaches, backed by isolated Genoese watchtowers, provide the main incentive to follow the Sentier des Douaniers (old custom officers' path) to this nature reserve.

8 Patrimonio

Some of Corsica's finest wines originate in the undulating chalk terrain of Patrimonio, where white cliffs frame views of the bay. The church is worth a look.

9 Centuri Port

Centuri's neatly painted fishermen's houses, set around the tiny harbour **(right)**, are truly picturesque. Its seafood restaurants keep the lobster boats busy.

NEED TO KNOW

MAP E2

Tourist Office: Port de Plaisance, Macinaggio; 04953 54034; www.macinaggiorogliano-capcorse.fr

Tourist Office: Place St Nicholas, Pietrabugno; 04955 42040; www.destination-cap-corse.com

Conservatoire du Cap Corse de Canari; 04953 78017; open Jun & Sep: 10am–noon & 2–5pm Mon–Fri, Jul & Aug: 10am–1pm & 4–8pm daily (Oct–Apr: call in advance)

▪ Nervous drivers should tour the cape's tortuous corniche clockwise. This ensures that they remain on the landward side of the road, away from drops. Going up the west coast in the morning and down the east coast in the afternoon also keeps the sun off you.

▪ Try the eponymous Cap Corse, a wine fortified with quinine (originally added as a malaria prophylaxis). Ask for "un Cap!"

TOP 10 ★ St-Florent and the Nebbio

The Col de Teghime (Teghime Pass), separating Bastia from the Golfe de St-Florent, marks a dramatic shift in landscape, from the flat, intensively cultivated east coast to the mountainous terrain of the Nebbio – Corsica's proverbial "Land of Mists". By the time you reach the compact resort of St-Florent itself, with its formidable backdrop of hills, the transition is complete. Press any further west and you venture into the Désert des Agriate, a sea of maquis and cacti fringed by empty beaches.

The Quayside
1 St-Florent's marina entices a steady flow of sailing enthusiasts over from the Riviera. This explains the odd Michelin star among the row of pizzerias lined up on the quayside fronting the harbour **(right)**.

2 Place des Portes
Pétanque, pastis and *passeghiata* – the "three Ps" – are the chief pastimes on offer in St-Florent's main square, where a trio of terrace cafés compete for custom in nonchalant Corsican style.

3 Plage du Loto
 Take a 15-minute boat cruise out across the gulf from St-Florent to the Plage du Loto **(above)**, where turquoise shallows and pure-white sand are patrolled by a herd of wild cows.

4 Citadelle
The bastion on the hillock above the harbour was built in 1439, bombarded by Nelson's fleet in 1794 and restored in 2000. The terrace has great views of the gulf.

5 Désert des Agriate
Hire mountain bikes from Casta to explore the trails crisscrossing this moonscape of dried-up river beds, cacti and maquis-shrouded hills.

6 Plage de Saleccia
An hour-long hike from Loto brings you to this wilder beach. Take a boat ride or a swim (but watch out for tidal rips).

7 Tour de Mortella
This watchtower **(above)** on the western shore of the gulf was the one that inspired Nelson to build a string of lookalike "Martello Towers" along the southern coasts of Britain and Ireland.

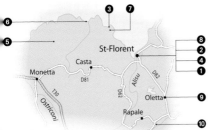

Map of St-Florent and the Nebbio

NELSON IN CORSICA

A forgotten naval campaign in Corsica provided future admiral Horatio Nelson with some valuable tactical lessons. Nelson was dispatched to the island in 1793 as part of Lord Hood's fleet, charged with supporting Pascal Paoli's insurrection against the French. The attack on the garrison at St-Florent went well enough, but Calvi proved a much tougher nut to crack – eventually costing Nelson the sight of one eye.

8 Santa Maria Assunta

Stroll up the lane from the square to reach the Pisan Church of Santa Maria Assunta. Inside its honey-coloured walls is a glass-sided coffin with the relics of St Flor, a Roman soldier.

9 Oletta

Pisan sculpture embellishes the façade of the 18th-century Église St-André in Oletta, a typical Nebbio village set high in the hills.

10 San Michele de Murato

Perched on a high terrace at the head of the Nebbio, this 12th-century chapel (see p43) features chequered bands of green schist and creamy yellow marble (below). Look out for the grotesque figures adorning the eaves.

NEED TO KNOW

MAP E3

Tourist Office: Bâtiment Administratif, Route Principale 53, 20217; 04953 70604; www.corsica-saintflorent.com

Santa Maria Assunta: 800 m (half a mile) northeast of Place des Portes (city centre); open Jun–Oct: 9:30am–noon Mon–Sat, 3–6:30pm Mon–Fri & Sun; at other times, ask at the tourist office in St-Florent for the key; adm €1.50, €2 for audio tour

Plage du Luto Boat Cruise: Le Popeye, promenade en mer, Campo d'Elge, St-Florent; 04953 71907; www.lepopeye. com; Cap Corse excursions €16, return trip to Plage du Loto €16 (€20 mid-Jul–Aug), for reservations call 06621 62376

■ Visit Corse Plaisance, south of the St-Florent city centre, for holiday basics.

■ Patisseries here sell *bastelles* (pasties filled with caramelized onions) or *blêtes* (pasties with chard spinach and cheese).

TOP 10 ★ Calvi

Calvi has been a ritzy seaside resort since the 1920s, when aristocratic refugees from the Côte d'Azur came to pursue illicit affairs in clubs such as the legendary Chez Tao. Rising straight from the waves, Calvi's Citadelle is easily the most imposing of Genoa's former strongholds, presiding over the bay. The icing on the cake, though, are the mountains. In clear weather, the snow-streaked Corsican watershed seems so close you could almost touch it.

1 Quai Landry
Café-restaurants line the ritzy Quai Landry, **(above)** and upstage even those of St Tropez and Cannes. If à la carte is pricey, buy a coffee and people-watch.

2 La Citadelle
Built in the 13th century, this imposing stone fortress houses the St-Jean-Baptiste cathedral, the Tour du Sel (where salt tax was levied) and the Maison Colombe, a derelict cottage controversially claimed to be the birthplace of Columbus.

3 Calvi Beach
Backed by a shady pine forest, Calvi's beach arcs in a picturesque curve of pale-orange sand and turquoise water around the gulf's southern rim. It's the ideal spot for relaxing.

4 Ste-Marie Majeure
The 17th-century belfry of Ste-Marie Majeure **(below)**, built in the Baroque style, dominates the backstreets of Calvi's old town, where restaurant tables spill across terraces on a square in summer. The city's Good Friday parade starts here.

5 Calvi Marina
Some of the gleaming yachts in this marina **(above)** have to be seen to be believed. The harbour pier affords splendid views of the waterfront and Citadelle.

6 St-Jean-Baptiste
This 13th-century octagonal-domed cathedral is the focal point of Calvi's Citadelle. A crucifix that allegedly saw off the Turkish siege of 1553 is its prized possession.

7 Calenzana
At the start of the GR20 (see p56) mountain trail, this village inland from Calvi centres on the Baroque Église St-Blaise, noted for its 17th-century tabernacle.

Map of Calvi

CLAIM TO FAME

Calvi's insistence that it, not Genoa, was the birthplace of Christopher Columbus rests on some shaky evidence: a family of weavers named "Colombu" did indeed live in the bastion while it served as a Genoese stronghold (Columbus' parents were definitely weavers). Additionally, the mariner named several New World settlements after Corsican saints and villages, and he allegedly kept his Corsican heritage a secret because of Calvi's rough reputation. On the strength of such scraps the town has declared the great explorer as its mascot.

8 The Trinighellu

Calvi's single-carriage tramway train (see p106), known as U Trinighellu (little train), rattles several times daily along the beautiful Balagne coast as far as L'Île Rousse. It stops at a string of pretty beaches, as well as at some off-the-beaten-track resorts.

9 Notre Dame de la Serra

The ultimate viewpoint over Calvi and its splendid gulf is from the terrace of this atmospheric hilltop church **(left)**. Readily accessible, it can be reached either in an hour's walk from the seafront or by car via a backroad off the D81.

10 Lumio

High up on the hillside, on the opposite side of the gulf from Calvi, is the picturesque village of Lumio **(above)**, site of San Pietro, a Romanesque Pisan chapel founded in the 11th century.

NEED TO KNOW

MAP B4 ■ Tourist Office: Port de Plaisance, 97 Chemin de la plage; 04956 51667; www.balagne-corsica.com

La Citadelle: Quai Landry, ville haute; 04956 59291

Maison Colombe: Rue Del-Filo; 04956 51667; visit by appt only

Ste-Marie-Majeure: between Rue Clémenceau and Blvd Wilson, ville basse; 04956 54252; open 8am–6pm

St-Jean-Baptiste: Citadelle; open 9am–7pm

■ The local train, U Trinighellu (www.train-corse.com), is a good way to reach one of the area's loveliest and least crowded beaches, plage de Bodri, 5 km (3 miles) west of L'Île Rousse (see p62).

■ A market offering fresh local produce is held every morning in the summer in the hall between Rue Clémenceau and Boulevard Wilson.

TOP 10 ⭐ Corte and its Hinterland

With its 18th- and 19th-century buildings and spectacular mountain setting, Corte presents a very different aspect of the island from the Mediterranean chic prevailing on the coast. As the seat of Pascal Paoli's independent parliament, this was the crucible of Corsican nationalism. A strong sense of the island's cultural distinctiveness still pervades the streets here, especially during term time, when Corsican-speaking students crowd the café terraces. Close by, some awesome landscapes lie within easy reach – you can walk out of the centre and be in a complete wilderness within an hour.

2 Cours Paoli
Lined with slightly dilapidated yet charming buildings, Corte's main thoroughfare is a legacy of its pivotal role in the Paoli era. It is full of bars, restaurants and shops; the cafés at the south end are the liveliest during school term.

3 Treasure Hunt
Discover Corte's history and hidden architectural gems on a self-guided "treasure hunt" organized by the Altipiani agency. You'll need the help of locals to crack the clues.

1 Vallée de la Restonica
A road from Corte runs to this valley (above). Jump on the shuttle bus in summer to reach Bergeries de Grotelle (shepherds' stone huts) and the lakes beyond.

4 Vallée du Tavignano
A wild, deep trench from Corte to the fringes of the watershed, the Vallée du Tavignano shelters pine forests and huge gorges. Access it by walking a cobbled Genoese mule trail.

5 Église de l'Annonciation
Joseph Bonaparte, Napoleon's elder brother, was christened in this mid-15th-century church (above) on place Gaffori. One of Corte's oldest buildings, this church houses a wax statue of St Theophilus, the town's much-loved patron saint.

6 Citadelle
Perched on top of a near-vertical crag, the town's Citadelle (left) is worth a visit for the views from its terraces over the crumbling *haute ville* and mountains.

Map of Corte

8 miles (5 miles)

RUE COLONEL FERACCI

COURS PAOLI

PL DES ARMES

PLACE PAOLI

R DU PROFESSEUR SANTIAGGI

AV PRES PERUCCI

15 km (9.3 miles)

8 Oratoire St-Théophile

The Franciscan monk and freedom fighter Blaise de Signori, better known as St Theophilus, was the first and only Corsican to be canonized. He is honoured with this chapel sited close to his birthplace in the Citadelle.

9 The Belvedere

Clamber up a flight of ancient stone steps beneath the ramparts of the Citadelle to reach this popular vantage point for panoramic views of the surrounding mountains.

7 Place Gaffori

Walls still pockmarked by musket fire from the 1740s set the tone of this picturesque square in Corte's *haute ville* (upper town). A statue of independence hero, General Gaffori, points stridently skywards **(above)**.

10 Musée de la Corse

Corte's cutting-edge museum showcases the island's traditional culture with exhibitions on farming, shepherding, religious brotherhoods, tourism and music. Your ticket also includes entry to the adjacent Citadelle.

NEED TO KNOW

MAP D6 ■ Tourist Office: La Citadelle; 04954 62670; www. corte-tourisme.com

Altipiani: 2 Place Paoli; 09603 70842; adm €10; www.altipiani-corse.com

Musée de la Corse and Citadelle: Citadelle, haute ville; 04954 52545; open Apr–mid-Jun: 10am–6pm Tue–Sun; mid-Jun–mid-Sep: 10am–8pm daily; mid-Sep–Oct: 10am–6pm Tue–Sun; Nov–Mar: 10am–5pm Tue–Sat; closed first 2 wks Jan; adm €5.30; www.musee-corse.com

■ For a perfect picnic location near the centre of Corte, head down the Avenue du Président Perucci and turn right just before the bridge to reach a pretty riverside spot behind the Citadelle.

■ Casanova, on the corner of Cours Paoli and Avenue Xavier Luciani, sells freshly baked local specialities.

TOP 10 ★ Golfe de Porto

The combination of red porphyry and lapis-blue sea have made the Golfe de Porto Corsica's defining landscape. No other place in the Mediterranean boasts such a striking juxtaposition, which is all the more astonishing for its backdrop of high mountains. From May to September, visitors come in thousands to marvel at the Calanche rocks, or to take boat trips to the Réserve Naturelle de Scandola. However, even at the height of summer it is possible to avoid the crowds by taking to the network of paved mule trails through the gulf's forested hinterland, or heading for the area's lesser-known coves.

1 Porto's Watchtower

Dwarfed by the cliffs that surround it, this 16th-century watchtower **(left)** offers fine views up the valley. A museum at the tower's base focuses on its history and the heather shrub.

2 Plage de Porto

Broad, steeply sloping and covered in dusty grey pebbles, this is not the most inspiring beach in the area, but it does make for a very scenic swim.

3 Porto

The scent of eucalyptus pervades Porto's harbour **(left)**, beneath immense cliffs. It is an ideal base for trips around the bay.

NEED TO KNOW

Porto Tourist Office:
MAP B6; Porto Marina; 04952 61055; www.porto-tourisme.com

Piana Tourist Office:
MAP A7; Place de la Mairie; 09669 28422

Porto Watchtower & Musée de la Bruyère:
MAP B6; Porto Marina;

04952 610 05; open Apr–Sep: 9am–7pm; adm €6.50

Boat Trips from Porto Marina: Porto Linea, 04952 22863, 06081 68971, www.portolinea.com; Nave Va, 04952 61516, 06171 16341, www.naveva.com

■ For a perfect car-free daytrip, take the boat to Girolata and walk up

to the Col de la Croix *(see p82)* in time to catch the twice-daily bus back to Porto (summer only; check timings at any tourist office).

■ Sip a chilled Muscat on the terrace of Les Roches Rouges in Piana, in the late afternoon when the views are at their best.

4 Boat Trips
A flotilla of excursion launches leaves Porto Marina daily in summer for fishing trips and tours of the gulf via its rock formations, sea caves and red cliffs.

Map of Golfe de Porto

6 Calanche Walks
The corniche wriggles through the centre of the world-famous rocks. To see the real highlights, follow one of the trails outlined in leaflets on sale at the tourist offices in Porto and Piana.

7 Capo d'Orto
The region's ultimate viewpoint is the domed summit of a vast sugar-loaf mountain, whose north face looms above Porto. A trail leads you to the top and back in around five hours.

8 The Corniche
This is Corsica's model coastal drive, but it can be a frustrating stop-and-start experience in the summer. Begin your journey in the early morning, when it's quiet and the light brings the red porphyry to life.

DRAGUT IN GIROLATA

Turgut Reis (1485–1565), a Greek-Ottoman admiral and privateer known as "Dragut", was the scourge of the Mediterranean in the 16th century. In 1540, he and his fleet were caught by the Genoese in Girolata. Dragut was in captivity for four years until his fellow corsair, Barabossa, forced his release, whereupon he promptly captured the town of Bonifacio. In 45 years at sea, Dragut captured more than 80 cities, towns and islands.

5 Piana
Occupying a prime position on the island, Piana **(above)** sits on a high natural balcony surveying the gulf. Stop in for a drink at the Les Roches Rouges hotel to enjoy superb views in sumptuous *fin-de-siècle* style.

9 Plage de Gradelle
Hardly anyone seems to know about this secluded pebble cove on the north-ern shore of the gulf **(right)**, reached via a backroad off the main corniche. Magnificent views across the water are its chief attraction.

10 Girolata
The most picturesque village on the island, Girolata lies beneath the salmon-pink cliffs of Scandola. It can be reached on foot from Col de la Croix **(left)** or by boat from Porto.

The Top 10
of Everything

The Îles Lavezzi, in the
Straits of Bonifacio

🔟 Moments in History

1 1077: Corsica Becomes a Pisan Protectorate

To rein in the feuding local warlords who refused to swear allegiance to the Church, the Pope placed Corsica under Pisan "protection" – a state of affairs repeatedly challenged by rival Genoa. Some 300 Romanesque chapels survive on the island from the Pisan occupation.

The Battle of Meloria

2 1284: The Battle of Meloria

Genoa's naval victory over Pisa at the Battle of Meloria saw it wrest control of Corsica from its long-standing adversary. One of the most successful rebels of this era was the nobleman Sinucello della Rocca, nicknamed "Giudice" (the Judge), for his legendary sense of fair play.

3 1564: Sampiero Corso's Rebellion

Having gained a toe-hold on the island under an alliance with Henry II of France, the Corsican-born mercenary Sampiero Corso led a succession of uprisings against the Genoese, aided by the local lords. He died in a vendetta killing 3 years later at the hands of his wife's brothers.

4 1736: Theodore von Neuhof Uprising

This 8-month interlude, during which the German adventurer Theodore von Neuhof set himself up as "King of Corsica", ended after a couple of ineffectual sieges exposed his lack of military expertise and funds.

5 1755: Paoli Returns to Corsica

Son of an exiled nationalist hero, Pascal Paoli made a triumphant return to Corsica to spearhead a full-scale rebellion. Coins were minted, an elected assembly and printing press were set up in the new capital, Corte, and a liberal constitution was put in place. Meanwhile, Genoa ceded its territorial rights to France.

The Battle of Ponte Nuovo

6 1769: The Battle of Ponte Nuovo

French forces slaughtered Paoli's ragtag army of patriots in a one-sided encounter on the Golo river. In its wake, resistance to French rule rapidly crumbled and Corsica became a fully integrated part of the French Republic, which it has remained ever since.

Statue of Sampiero Corso

7 1943: Liberation of Corsica

Hastened by the Allied invasion of southern Italy, Field Marshal Kesselring was forced to withdraw his Nazi forces from Corsica via Bastia. The Corsican Resistance, or Maquis, fought the retreating Germans with great spirit, inspiring their counterparts on the mainland.

Fighters of the Corsican Resistance

8 1975: The Siege of Aléria

A cell of Corsican nationalist paramilitaries took over the Depeille wine cellar near Aléria to protest against fraudulent wine-making practices by Algerian immigrants. In the ensuing shoot-out, two policemen died. The event marked the start of armed resistance against French rule.

9 1998: The Murder

Préfet Claude Érignac, the most senior French official in Corsica, was shot by a maverick nationalist gunman in Ajaccio. The atrocity galvanized attempts to resolve the armed conflict, which left hundreds dead.

10 2015: Corsican Nationalist Movement

Since the 1960s, the nationalist movement in Corsica has campaigned for more autonomy, if not full independence. The nationalists gained significant political success when Gilles Simeoni's pro-autonomy coalition, Pè a Corsica, won the French regional elections in 2015.

TOP 10 HISTORICAL FIGURES

1 Sampiero Corso (1498–1567)
A flamboyant Corsican warlord, who is thought by some to have inspired Shakespeare's *Othello*.

2 Dragut (1485–1565)
One of the most feared pirates in history, Dragut was captured in Girolata.

3 Marthe Franceschini (1756–99)
Daughter of Corsican parents abducted by pirates in 1754, Marthe became the Queen of Morocco in 1786.

4 Theodore von Neuhof (1694–1756)
The much maligned "operetta king" from Westphalia, who ruled Corsica for eight months.

5 Gian Petro Gaffori (1704–53)
Corsican military commander who led the 1750s revolt against Genoese rule.

6 Pascal Paoli (1725–1807)
The founding father of independent Corsica and author of the Constitution.

7 Sir Gilbert Elliot (1751–1814)
Viceroy of Corsica during the Anglo-Corsican interlude of 1794.

8 Napoleon Bonaparte (1769–1821)
Born Napoleone Buonaparte in Ajaccio in 1769, the Emperor loathed the island of his birth.

9 Danielle Casanova (1909–43)
Corsican-born heroine of the French Resistance, who died in Auschwitz.

10 Max (b. 1929) and Edmond Simeoni (b. 1934)
Masterminds of the Aléria siege of 1975, which kick-started the nationalist armed struggle in Corsica.

Portrait of Napoleon Bonaparte

Prehistoric Sites

① U Nativu, Patrimonio
MAP E3

In a shelter just south of Patrimonio church stands a superb statue-menhir known as "U Nativu", dating from 900–800 BC. The statue bears distinct facial features and a T-shaped breastbone. Its sombre face has become something of a mascot for this famous wine-producing area. In July, it is also given pride of place at the village's guitar festival.

② Alignement de Palaggiu
MAP J6

Most of the 258 menhirs at this extraordinary site *(see p19)* date from 1800 BC. The grandfather of Corsican archaeology, Roger Grosjean, asserted that they must have functioned as some kind of deterrent to would-be invaders because of their proximity to the coast. Whatever their origins, the stones still cast an undeniably eerie spell. To get to them, look for the turning just after the Mosconi vineyard on the left.

③ Filitosa

This privately owned site *(see p16)* in southwest Corsica has earned UNESCO World Heritage status for its statue-menhirs, many featuring skilfully carved faces and daggers – a trait of the island's Torréen population, who lived here nearly 4,000 years ago. Do visit the small museum.

Statue-menhirs of Filitosa

④ Castellu d'Araggio

This marvellous Torréen site *(see p88)*, high in the hills north of Porto-Vecchio, dates from 1500 BC and has traces of prehistoric cooking fires. The views alone are worth a detour, and there is a pleasant café, Orée du Site, at the start of the path.

The verdant Pianu di Levie

⑤ Pianu di Levie (Cucuruzzu)

A fairy-tale woodland of twisted oaks and mossy boulders enfolds the magical Pianu di Levie *(see p85)* whose *pièce de résistance*, Cucuruzzu, is a well-preserved Torréen castle dating from around 1400 BC – complete with living chambers and slab roofs. A second site, Capula, lies a 20-minute walk away. Kids will adore this hugely atmospheric location.

⑥ Site Archéologique de Cauria

Filitosa is more famous, but two of the menhirs at Stantari are the equal of their high-profile cousins in Valinco, with well-sculpted features, diagonal swords and sockets in their heads where horns must once have been. The Dolmen de Fontanaccia and Alignements de Palaggiu and Rinaghju are in the same area *(see p18)*.

7 Musée Départemental de Préhistoire Corse et d'Archéologie, Sartène

This collection *(see p18)* of prehistoric artifacts from all over Corsica is dominated by Neolithic pottery fragments, obsidian arrowheads and polished stone axes, but also includes pieces of gold jewellery and strings of coloured glass beads that look as fresh as the day they were buried.

8 Dolmen de Fontanaccia
MAP J6

A granite structure *(see p19)* dating from the late megalithic period, when bodies, previously interred in stone coffins, were buried in stone chambers and covered in compacted earth. Lost in the depths of the Sartenais region, this chamber ranks among the best preserved in southern Europe. Its former contents now reside in the museum at Sartène.

Stone burial chamber, Sartène

9 The Pieve Menhirs
MAP E4

It is well worth making the scenic trip to this little-frequented village in the hills overlooking St-Florent to see its three statue-menhirs, which stand together on a terrace of raised ground next to the church. The family group, chiselled some 3,500 years ago from local granite, appear to be gazing wistfully over the valley, perhaps admiring the fabulous views.

10 Musée de l'Alta Rocca, Levie

MAP K4 ■ Ave Lieutenant de Peretti, Quartier Pratu, Levie ■ Guided tours and reservations: 04957 80078 ■ Open Oct–May: 10am–5pm Tue–Sat; Jun–Sep: 10am–6pm daily ■ Closed public hols ■ Adm

This museum in Levie has a single prize exhibit: a human skeleton dating from 6570 BC, known as "La Dame de Bonifacio" (or "La Dame d'Araguina"). The woman died in her mid-30s and is thought to have been disabled by severely fractured legs. Also look out for the skeleton of the now extinct rabbit rat.

La Dame de Bonifacio, Levie

Churches and Cathedrals

Interior of St-Jean-Baptiste, Bastia

1 St-Jean-Baptiste, Bastia

MAP P5 ▪ 4 Rue du Cardinal
Viale Prela, Place de l'Hôtel-de-Ville
▪ 0495 55 24 60 ▪ Open Mon–Sat &
10:30am Sun for Mass only ▪ www.
saintjeanbaptiste-bastia.fr

With twin belfries and a Neo-Classical façade, Corsica's largest church lends a typically Italian feel to the former Genoese harbour. The lavish rococo interior features gilt stucco, rare marble and trompe-l'oeil paintings.

2 La Canonica, near Bastia

Set on Bastia's southern fringes, this Romanesque cathedral *(see p23)* was built in the early 12th century, on the site of a 4th-century basilica which was destroyed by successive invasions. The Corinthian columns are thought to have come from the Roman settlement that once stood opposite it.

3 Oratoire de Monserato, Bastia

MAP F5 ▪ Route de Saint-Florent
▪ Open 10am–6pm daily

Cleanse yourself of all sins as you ascend the Scala Santa in Bastia's famous Oratoire de Monserato

(see p23). Only penitents willing to make the pilgrimage on their knees may approach the altar at the top of the staircase, a privilege granted by the Pope.

4 Oratoire de l'Immaculée Conception, Bastia

MAP P5 ▪ Rue Napoléon ▪ Open daily

Dating from 1589, this church *(see p22)* has witnessed innumerable civic events in its time, including the initiation of the colonial governors. It was also where the British Viceroy, Sir Gilbert Elliot *(see p39)*, once pre-sided over the island's parliament. The interior is filled with velvet drapes and lashings of gold leaf.

5 Santa Maria Assunta, St-Florent

Santa Maria Assunta *(see p29)* ranks alongside La Canonica as the finest surviving Pisan edifice on the island. With enigmatic carvings of writhing serpents and wild animals, its arched entrance reveals a Baroque interior housing the mummified remains of Roman centurian St Flor.

Picturesque St-Martin, Patrimonio

6 St-Martin, Patrimonio

MAP E3

Now the symbol of the famous wine-growing region, St-Martin's bare, brown, schist campanile crowns the top of a wooded hillock and looks magnificent against the surrounding vineyards and chalk hills. Do not miss the famous limestone statue-menhir "U Nativu" below it, which seems to be singing or howling.

⑦ San Michele de Murato
MAP E4

San Michele's trademark chequered pattern, rendered in grey-green serpentine and off-white marble, entices a steady stream of admirers. Dating from the 12th century, the church (see p29) preserves a wealth of reliefs of peculiar carved beasts and human figures – typical of the Pisan period. It is also one of the few medieval shrines still with its belfry.

Fresco, Église de la Trinité, Aregno

look exactly like its contemporary, San Michele de Murato, in a chequered pattern of green and cream blocks. Rising from the edge of Aregno, this church is encrusted with wonderful allegorical carvings of mythical beasts and folk figures. The most famous of these, crowning the apex, depicts a man clasping his foot and is thought to symbolize the affliction of sin.

⑩ Chapelle Ste-Christine, Cervione, Valle di Campoloro
MAP F6 ■ 04953 81140

This Romanesque chapel has twin apses nestled on a terrace overlooking the east coast near Cervione which retain late 15th-century frescoes rendered in vibrant, earthy hues. Its patron, Saint Christina, is depicted next to a kneeling monk. The chapel is signposted off the D71 and is only a short way from Cervione on the left.

Exterior of San Michele de Murato

⑧ St-Jean-Baptiste, Calvi

Founded in the 13th century, Calvi's honey-coloured cathedral had to be rebuilt after the Turkish siege of 1553, when its principal statue – Christ des Miracles – was brandished from the ramparts to repel the attackers (see pp30–31). The statue now enjoys pride of place in a chapel to the right of the choir.

⑨ Église de la Trinité et de San Giovanni, Aregno
MAP C4

This 12th-century Pisan masterpiece was built to

Pretty Villages

The picturesque clifftop village of Montemaggiore

1 Montemaggiore
MAP C4

Montemaggiore straggles over a rocky ridge inland from Calvi, its ancient, buttressed-walled tower houses huddled around a church tower that is dwarfed by the intimidating bulk of Monte Grosso behind. For the best views, climb the outcrop at the eastern entrance to the village, known locally as "A Cima".

Great views of Ste-Lucie de Tallano

2 Ste-Lucie de Tallano
MAP K5

The orange-tiled rooftops of this Alta Rocca village *(see p17)*, spread over a high balcony looking across the Rizzanese Valley to the Sartenais coast, are a magical sight from higher up the mountain. The village's 18th-century centre ranges around a square where you can have wood-baked pizzas next to a fountain.

3 Morosaglia
MAP E5

This tiny village in the Castagniccia region is where Pascal Paoli *(see p39)* was born, and where his ashes are enshrined in a marble-lined chapel. From its fringes, where a couple of Romanesque churches hide in the maquis, chestnut forest gives way to a panorama of high ridges.

4 Zonza
MAP K4

One of the most clichéd images of the Corsican interior is that of Zonza, framed by the unmistakable Aiguilles de Bavella. This village, where Muhammed V, Sultan of Morocco, was exiled in 1952, lies a long trek from the granite peaks, but it is no less picturesque for all that, especially after a rare dusting of Mediterranean snow.

5 Santa-Lucia-di-Mercurio
MAP E6

The best reason to drive out to Santa-Lucia-di-Mercurio, on the south side of the Vallée du Tavignano *(see p32)* in the Bozio region of central Corsica, is to admire it from a distance. Connoisseurs of great views will revel in the sight of its campanile and slate-roofed cottages set against the pale-grey crags and melting snow fields of distant Monte Rotondo.

6 Ota

Before Porto's development as a tourist hub (see p34), Ota was the gulf area's principal village, and remains a far more charming spot. The rear terraces of its bars enjoy superb vistas across to Capo d'Orto's cliffs (see p35), while the Tra Mare e Monti Nord trail (see p57) leads to some stunning viewpoints.

7 Tralonca
MAP D6

Perched on the top of a conical hill on the opposite side of the valley from Corte, Tralonca lies about as far off the tourist trail as it is possible to get in Corsica. The village warrants a detour for its pretty core of square cottages, packed around a Baroque church amid miles of terraced fields.

8 Evisa

Midway between the Golfe de Porto (see pp34–5) and Col de Vergio (see p80), the village of Evisa (see p81) is swathed in chestnut forest. Paved mule paths dating from the Genoese era lead down pretty woodland walks to secluded swimming spots, and the local restaurants excel in traditional mountain cuisine.

Wooden statue along chestnut trail

9 Sant'Antonino

Situated at the summit of a conical hill in the Balagne region of northwest Corsica, the village of Sant'Antonino (see p100) is the oldest inhabited settlement on the island. Its narrow vaulted alleyways and cobbled lanes have not undergone much change since the time of the Savelli lords, who ruled from here in the 9th century.

10 Pigna

On the back of a very successful restoration project, these formerly run-down medieval houses have become beautifully renovated into a chocolate-box vision of neat stonework and blue-painted doors and window shutters. This thriving cobblestoned village, located in the Nervia valley (see p99), has become famous for its traditional Corsican music and arts and crafts, with artisans steadily working away in its workshops.

Watchtowers and Lighthouses

1 Tour d'Agnello
MAP E1

Atop a high promontory on the north coast of Cap Corse, this tower is a great vantage point over this wild and beautiful stretch of coast. Follow the path away from Barcaggio village for about 45 minutes, and try to visit in spring, when wild flowers carpet the surrounding clifftops.

2 Tour de Pinarellu
MAP L5

Rising from the crest of a low headland just north of Porto-Vecchio, this watchtower completes the perfect sweep of Pinarellu beach – a popular family hang-out in summer, where veterans of the infamous GR20 mountain trail come to ease their feet.

3 Tour de Santa Maria, Cap Corse
MAP E1

This tower is one of 91 structures erected by the Genoese in the 15th and 16th centuries as an early warning system against pirates. Cleft in half, Santa Maria cuts a forlorn figure at the far end of a bay of blue water, surrounded by vineyards, maquis and rolling hills.

Tour de Santa Maria, Cap Corse

4 Tour de Capo Rosso
MAP A7

This spectacularly sited watchtower crowns a majestic red granite mountain at the southwest tip of the Golfe de Porto. Cliffs fall away to churning sea on three sides, while to the east a remarkable view unfolds over the

bay to the high peaks inland. The trail starts 7 km (4 miles) west of Piana on the D824.

5 Tour de la Parata
MAP G3

The 12-m (39-ft) high Tour de la Parata dates from 1608. Its profile, rising from the top of a pyramidal headland at the northwestern tip of the Golfe d'Ajaccio, is echoed by that of the nearby Îles Sanguinaires (see p12), receding like stepping stones out to sea. The house of Parata is home to a tourist office and a médiathèque (multimedia library).

6 Tour de Capo di Muro
MAP H4

Although less than an hour's drive from Ajaccio, Capo di Muro is as wild a promontory as any on the island.

Locals wishing to get away from it all come here for a windy walk, heading down a rough path through the maquis to the tower crowning the headland's crest.

7 Tour de Campomoro
MAP H5 ■ Exposition Barbaresques: mid Apr–Sep: 9am–4:30pm; adm

The largest watchtower on the island, the 15 m (49 ft) Tour de Campomoro presides over a picture-perfect bay and contains Exposition Barbaresques, an exhibition on the history of Corsica's watchtowers. Behind the tower lies a deserted shore, where bleached granite boulders have been eroded into extraordinary shapes. The path continues to Roccapina.

8 Tour de Senetosa
MAP H6

Put on your hiking shoes and trek a couple of hours through dense juniper scrub and myrtle bushes to reach the Tour de Senetosa. Built of white granite, it sits astride a rocky ridge next to a wind-powered lighthouse, overlooking a string of remote beaches. Pick up the path to it in Tizzano, and take along plenty of water.

9 Tour de Mortella, Désert des Agriate
MAP E3

Nelson was so impressed with the Tour de Mortella when he attacked it in 1794 that he copied its design for a chain of structures along the southern

Tour de Mortella, Désert des Agriate

shores of Britain – the so-called "Martello Towers" *(see p29)*. Visible from the excursion boats running to nearby Plage du Loto, it can only be reached on foot via the coast path.

10 Phare de Pertusato
MAP K7

The most southerly spit of land in France, Capo Pertusato lies an hour's walk over the cliff tops from Bonifacio. Its lighthouse was constructed in 1838 to safeguard shipping in what still ranks among the most treacherous seaways in Europe. A stunning view over the Îles Lavezzi and Sardinia extends from the headland.

Lighthouse on Capo Pertusato

TOP 10 Natural Wonders

The stunning White Cliffs of Bonifacio are best viewed from a boat

1 The White Cliffs of Bonifacio

MAP K7

Seagulls swarm above Bonifacio's corrugated chalk escarpments. The cliffs are so eroded at their base that they seem on the verge of collapse – which they have done in places, as shown by chunks of fallen debris. See them at their most striking on a boat trip out of the harbour.

2 Aiguilles de Bavella

A phalanx of seven mighty pinnacles soaring over a carpet of pine forest, the needle-shaped peaks of Bavella *(see p87)* look like a vision from a fantasy novel. Whether viewed up close from

Madonna statue, Aiguilles de Bavella

the waymarked scrambling routes around their bases, or from the white Madonna statue at the Col, the needles present a truly breathtaking spectacle.

3 Laricio Pines, Forêt d'Aïtone

Some venerable old Laricio pines surviving in Forêt d'Aïtone reach a height of 50 m (164 ft), making them the tallest conifers in Europe *(see p80)*. The Genoese used to prize the trees as ships' masts but they are now protected.

4 Scandola

Accessible only by sea, the terracotta headland at the northwest entrance to the Golfe de Porto *(see p53)* is the most heavily protected land in France – a precious wild habitat and spectacular geological oddity. Experience the magical sea caves, giant sea eagles' nests and porphyry rock formations around its fringes on a boat excursion out of Porto's marina.

5 L'Oriu de Canni

MAP K6

Shaped like a witch's hat, this rock, rising above the tiny hamlet of Cani, is associated with all manner of spooky tales. Children will love its enigmatic appearance when the shadows lengthen in late afternoon. Cani lies 20 km (12 miles) southwest of Porto-Vecchio, near the village of Chera on the D59.

7 Paglia Orba
MAP C6

Soaring above the Vallée de Niolo *(see p94)*, Paglia Orba, at 2,525 m (8,284 ft), is one of Corsica's highest mountains and a most distinctive peak, with a shark's-fin shape. The ascent – a 2-hour scramble from Ciottulu a i Mori refuge at its foot – is simpler than it looks from below.

8 Spelunca Gorge

Towering cliffs flank this deep valley *(see p78)*, which snakes inland from Porto to the Col de Vergio pass into the Niolo region. Natural pools in the river at its base offer plenty of swimming spots with views.

9 Grouper

Slow-moving and faintly comical with their prominent lips, grouper *(mérou)* are the stars of the Corsican underwater world. Divers queue in the Bouches de Bonifacio *(see p53)* to visit one colony of fishes that are tame enough to touch.

10 Calanche de Piana
MAP B7

The contorted orange granite of the Calanche de Piana covers the mountainside into the Golfe de Porto *(see pp34–5)*. The corniche cuts through the Calanche, giving access to a network of way-marked trails. While most are easily viewed from the road, some of the strangest rock formations can be seen on a boat trip from Porto.

6 Lac de Nino

Wild horses graze the green pastures surrounding this divine high-altitude lake *(see p96)*. A long, uphill walk is required to get here, but it is rewarded with the very first glimpse of the glass-like water, its surface reflecting the backdrop of snow-streaked peaks and ridges.

Lac de Nino, surrounded by mountains

🔟 Great Beaches

② Plage de Santa Giulia
MAP L6

If it weren't for the Corsican maquis and Mediterranean villas spread over the surrounding hills, this bay of dazzling aquamarine water and soft white sand could be mistaken for the Caribbean. The beach gets jam-packed in the school holidays, as it lies within an easy drive of Porto-Vecchio and many of the island's campsites.

Watersports at plage de Santa Giulia

③ Plage de Roccapina
MAP J6

A lion-shaped rock formation and watchtower overlook water as transparent and sand as soft as anywhere in the Mediterranean. The beach is accessed via a badly rutted track, which often keeps the crowds at arm's length. Climb the path up the headland to the north for a bird's-eye view of this secluded cove.

① Plage de Saleccia
MAP D3

The waters off Saleccia must be among the clearest in Corsica. Low rainfall in this desert area ensures minimal runoff from streams, leaving the shallows crystalline – perfect for snorkelling. The beach is as far-flung as it is beautiful. Camp in the site behind to enjoy seeing the sand turn red at sunrise and sunset.

Plage de Roccapina

Café overlooking plage de Cupabia

4 Plage de Cupabia
MAP H4

The sea at this glorious bay at the far northeastern end of the Golfe de Valinco can get choppy if there is a strong westerly wind. But in calm weather, the shallows are fine for kids to swim in. Facilities extend to a café, car park and basic campsite.

5 Plage de l'Ostriconi

Only a handful of visitors pull off the highway between Bastia and Calvi to enjoy this unspoiled, deserted bay (see p102). There are no facilities here, though wood chalets and camping spaces are available a little way inland.

6 Plage de Rondinara
MAP L6

A clam-shaped lagoon entered via a slim gap between two head-lands, this isolated bay between Porto-Vecchio and Bonifacio does not attract the crowds you'd expect given how lovely it is – except in peak season, when the campsite behind it fills up. Bring your snorkelling kit –the underwater life is prolific.

7 Plage de Petit Sperone
MAP K7

This hidden gem is tucked away at the southeasternmost tip of the island, below a complex of millionaires' retreats and an exclusive golf course. It is not even marked on IGN maps, but you can reach the cove via a foot-path from the beach at Piantarella nearby, where there is a rough lay-by to park in.

8 Plage d'Erbaju
MAP J6

Climb over the headland north of Roccapina and follow the track downhill to a spectacular 2-km (1-mile) sweep of coarse sand, with lots of space even at the height of summer. The chic Murtoli estate's rental cottages (see p112) are the only buildings visible for miles.

9 Plage de Palombaggia

Palombaggia's trio of gently shelving bays, lapped by shallow, turquoise water, are perfect for children. A row of stately umbrella pines provides shade in the dunes behind, and there is a terrific beach café at the southernmost cove – Le Tamaricciu (see p89) – serving gourmet snacks and cold chestnut beer. During the summer months, jump on the bus to get here from Porto-Vecchio (see p86).

Secluded plage de Palombaggia

10 Plage du Loto
MAP E3

Catch a boat from St-Florent to reach this splendid beach with shining white sand and clear turquoise sea water, tucked away on the Désert des Agriates' pristine, rocky coast. The views across the gulf to the mountains of Cap Corse are unforgettable.

🔟 Boat Trips

Girolata and Réserve Naturelle de Scandola

1 Girolata and Réserve Naturelle de Scandola

MAP A6 ▪ Via Mare, Porto Marina ▪ 06072 87272 ▪ www.viamare-promenades.com

A fleet of excursion boats chugs out of Porto's Marina during the summer, shuttling visitors out to the famous Réserve Naturelle de Scandola, with its soaring red cliffs. Boats stop for lunch at Girolata.

2 Golfe d'Ajaccio

MAP H3 ▪ Nave Va, Port Tino Rossi, Ajaccio ▪ 04955 13131 ▪ www.naveva.com

Ajaccio looks dazzling when viewed from the bay. Boats leave Port Tino Rossi daily in summer for trips along the Rive Sud to Bonifacio, passing by Capo di Muro (see p82). There is a stop for coffee and a swim en route.

3 Santa Teresa di Gallura

MAP K7 ▪ Moby Lines ▪ mid-Mar–Oct: daily ▪ www.mobylines.com

The ferry ride from Bonifacio to Santa Teresa di Gallura in the north of Sardinia is thrilling, affording superb views of the white cliffs of Bonifacio.

4 Îles Cerbicale

MAP L6 ▪ Chiocca Croisières, Porto Vecchio Harbour ▪ 04957 14150/03367 ▪ www.amour-des-iles.com

The highlight of boat trips from Porto-Vecchio's harbour are the Îles Cerbicale, an archipelago of islets rising from the turquoise waters off Plage de Palombaggia (see p87). Longer excursions continue on to Bonifacio and Îles Lavezzi, stopping for a dip at a secluded cove on the return leg.

5 Sea Kayak Guided Tours

MAP M1 ▪ 07812 54832 ▪ www.ussuk-kayak.com

USSUK offers private 4- to 7-day sea kayak tours around Corsica's most beautiful coasts. Some experience is necessary. Fees include equipment, an English- or French-speaking certified guide and a photo workshop.

6 Cap Corse

MAP F1 ▪ San Paulu, Port de Plaisance, Macinaggio Harbour ▪ 06147 81416 ▪ www.sanpaulu.com

Jump aboard the *San Paulu* in Macinaggio Marina for a jaunt along the beautiful north coast of Cap Corse. The boat anchors for lunch at Barcaggio village. Trips also run to the nearby Italian island of Capraia.

7 Îles Lavezzi

MAP L7 ▪ Marine de Bonifacio ▪ 04957 30117, 06863 40049 ▪ Thalassa boat trips: www.vedettesthalassa.com

The Îles Lavezzi are a cluster of low-lying islets in the Straits of

A boat sailing between the Îles Lavezzi

Bonifacio *(see p85)*. Boats shuttle to and from them throughout the day, leaving you time to snorkel amid some of the Mediterranean's marine life.

8 Plage du Loto
MAP E3 ■ Le Popeye, Campo d'Elge, St-Florent ■ 04953 71907
■ www.lepopeye.com

You'll never forget the first time you see beautiful Plage du Loto. A rolling ride across the gulf from St-Florent, the cove's brilliant turquoise waters remain hidden until you are almost upon them. Depart early and you'll have time to walk to Saleccia.

Rugged coastline of Golfe de Porto

9 Golfe de Porto
MAP A6 ■ Colombo Line ■ 049 56 53210 ■ www.colombo-line.com

Colombo Line takes you from Calvi's Quai Landry *(see p30)* around the northwest coast to the Réserve Naturelle de Scandola and Calanche in the Golfe de Porto *(see pp34–5)*. The boats stop at Girolata for a scenic lunch overlooking the beach.

10 Calanche de Piana
MAP B7 ■ Porto Linea
■ 04952 22863, 06081 68971
■ www.portolinea.com

The sea caves and volcanic rocks of the Calanche *(see p35)* feature on boat tours of the Golfe de Porto's southern shore. Boats run from Porto as far as the foot of Capo Rosso, while full-day sailings cross the bay to Scandola and Girolata *(see p35)*.

TOP 10 DIVE SITES

Underwater wreck of the B-17

1 B-17, Calvi
MAP B4
Shot down in 1944, this American bomber rests in the turquoise water.

2 Les Cathédrales et les Aiguilles, Golfe de Valinco
MAP J5
These underwater mountain ranges are inhabited by 60 species of fish.

3 Le Tonneau and Red Canyon, Golfe de Valinco
MAP J5
There is exceptional diving at this pair of deep-water sites.

4 Capo di Muro, Ajaccio
MAP H4
The most southerly point in the gulf has abundant sea life.

5 Le Banc Provençal, Golfe de Lava
MAP G2
An Aladdin's Cave of rainbow wrasse and multicoloured sea sponges.

6 Vardiola and Punta Mucchilina, Golfe de Porto
MAP A6
Coral is abundant at these two sites.

7 L'Ila Morsetta, Galéria
MAP B5
This giant underwater boulder choke teems with conger eels and lobster.

8 Mérouville, Bouches de Bonifacio
MAP K7
Large colonies of grouper are the main draw of this celebrated dive site.

9 Pain de Sucre and la Canonnière, Bastia
MAP F3
These impressive rock formations lurk in the seas just north of Bastia.

10 Le Danger du Toro, Porto-Vecchio
MAP L5
Cliffs plunge to 40 m (131 ft), where you can see red coral, grouper and an impressive canyon.

Outdoor Activities

1 Hiking
www.pnr.corsica

Take to the network of long-distance hiking trails to explore Corsica's rugged interior. Ranging from 2-day coastal ambles to the 2-week marathon of the GR20 *(see p56)*, the routes are all well equipped with hostels and huts.

2 Canyoning
www.corse-montagne.com

This adventure sport, which allows you to climb and abseil through stream gorges using ropes and harnesses, has caught on fast in Corsica. The island's side valleys offer many possibilities for outfits running guided trips.

3 Mountain Biking

The tracks winding through Corsica's magnificent forests and along the more open stretches of coast make for some superb rides. A very popular route is the 11-km (7-mile) cycle through the Désert des Agriate to Saleccia *(see p28)*.

4 Via Ferrata
www.viaferrata.org

Winding up spectacular rock faces and ridges, via ferratas enable climbers to navigate mountain routes without needing to use their own ropes.

5 Snorkelling and Diving
www.divingcorsica.com

Corsica's underwater topography is no less spectacular than the terrain on dry land, with sudden drops from sandy bottomed bays to blue voids nearly 1,000 m (3,300 ft) deep in some places. Multicoloured fish are a common sight while snorkelling, and dive prospects rank among the most exciting in Europe.

Divers off the coast of Corsica

6 Horse Riding
www.tourisme-equestre-corse.com

Riding a horse over a sandy beach and bathing the animal afterwards in transparent sea water is an experience few places in the world can offer. Bred to thrive in Corsica's rough terrain, local ponies await riders at a dozen or more equestrian centres dotted around the island.

Horse riding on the beach

A skier on the slopes at Ghisoni

⑦ Skiing
www.skiinfo.fr/corse/stations-de-ski.html

Corsica is not exactly known as a winter sports destination. However, if you happen to be on the island after a rare blizzard, join the exodus to the three surviving ski stations at Val d'Ese (northeast of Ajaccio), Vergio (Niolo) and E'Capannelle (Ghisoni).

⑧ Adventure Parks
A big craze in Corsica, areas of forest across the island have been equipped with cable bridges, aerial walkways and zip slides to create assault courses that really get your pulse racing (see p63).

⑨ Rock Climbing
http://escalade.corse.topo.free.fr

Corsica boasts a number of rock-climbing hot spots. The most famous of them are the Aiguilles de Bavella in the south, the red escarpments crenellating Paglia Orba (see p48) and the awe-inspiring north face of Capo d'Orto (see p35), near Porto on the west coast.

⑩ Kayaking
www.corsekayak.com

Beach hop along the wilder stretches of Corsica's coastline by rented kayak. Organized expeditions involve bivouacs in deserted coves and circumnavigating promontories such as Scandola and Capo Rosso. USSUK offers private kayaking (see p52) tours lasting several days for those who have some experience.

TOP 10 ULTIMATE VIEWS

1 Monte Cinto
MAP C6
On a clear day, you can see the distant Alps from Corsica's highest summit at 2,706 m (8,900 ft).

2 Monte Corona
MAP C5
See an astounding panorama from this mountaintop above Calenzana.

3 Notre-Dame-de-la-Serra
MAP B4
The views over the Golfe de Calvi from this hilltop chapel are magnificent.

4 Monte San Petrone
MAP E6
This peak offers views over the chestnut forests of Castagniccia (see p94).

5 Capo Rosso
MAP A7
Climb this headland for a vista over the Calanche and gulf to Paglia Orba.

6 Chemin des Crêtes
MAP H3
There are superb views over the capital and its gulf from this high path.

7 Tour de Roccapina
MAP J6
This tower overlooks a paradise cove and a vast empty beach of white sand.

8 Capo Pertusato
MAP K7
The culmination of Bonifacio's white cliffs gives a view across to Sardinia.

9 Foca Alta, Cartalavonu
MAP K5
This high pass in the Massif de l'Ospédale above Porto-Vecchio (see p86) overlooks the southwest coast.

10 Capo d'Orto
MAP B7
This domed peak provides a great vantage point over the Golfe de Porto.

View from Capo d'Orto

Treks and Walks

Hikers trekking the famous GR20 route in Autumn

1 GR20
MAP C5

Corsica's legendary high-altitude trek, tackled by around 18,000 people each year, ranks among the most challenging multi-stage itineraries in Europe. This tough 10-day adventure is not to be undertaken lightly.

Pont de Zaglia between Evisa and Ota

2 Evisa–Ota
MAP B7

This is a popular half-day walk through the fragrant chestnut forest that separates two of the island's prettiest hill villages. Tackle the paved Genoese mule track uphill from Ota or start in Evisa. Midway, the Pont de Zaglia spans a stream, and makes for a gorgeous picnic and swimming spot.

3 Mare a Mare Nord
MAP G1

A classic coast-to-coast route, this trail winds across the island at its widest point, via a parade of scenic highlights, including the Gorges du Tavignano and Vallée de Niolo *(see p94)*. This is among the lesser-visited long-distance paths.

4 Mare a Mare Sud
MAP J5

A 5-day traverse of the idyllic far south of the island, this trail is punctuated by *gîtes d'étapes* (lodges) where you can unwind after each stage. Landscapes vary from pristine oak forest to grassy uplands, with many swimming spots en route.

5 Campomorro–Roccapina
MAP H5

A terrific 2-day coastal hike along the rugged shoreline of the Sartenais *(see pp18–19)*, this route is peppered with beautiful coves and watchtowers. However, navigation can be tricky and there is very little shade or water along the route.

6 Sentier des Douaniers, Cap Corse
MAP F1

A 2-day coastal itinerary around the wild northern tip of Cap Corse *(see pp26–7)*, this trail takes in turquoise bays and scrubland. Starting at Macinaggio, it winds to Centuri Port, via an overnight stop at Barcaggio.

7 Sentier Littoral, Désert des Agriate
MAP D3

Three days are generally advised for this wild coastal hike along the edge of the Désert des Agriate *(see p28)*. There is a campsite at Saleccia and a refuge at Plage de Guigno, but there are no other facilities. In early summer you'll have the stunning beaches all to yourself.

(8) Tra Mare e Monti Nord
MAP B4

This is Corsica's second most popular walking route after the GR20 and takes you through the red-granite landscapes of the northwest. The pretty village of Girolata *(see p35)*, with its beaches and mountainous hinterland, is the route's highlight.

(9) Lacs de Melo et Capitello

The path up the grandiose Restonica valley to this pair of exquisite glacial lakes *(see p93)* gets jammed with hikers in high summer, but follow it in May or September and you are in for a treat. The reward is a vast amphitheatre of rock, scree and snow surrounding two shimmering blue lakes, formed at different altitudes.

(10) Trou de la Bombe
MAP L4

This family-friendly amble takes you through the soaring granite pinnacles and pine forests of Bavella en route to the famous *Trou* – a large hole created by wind erosion in a vast escarpment. Climb up for dizzying views down to the coast.

Trou de la Bombe

TOP 10 TREKKING TIPS

Signpost in a national park

1 Wild Camping
It is illegal to wild camp in Corsica, so plan your accommodation in advance.

2 Booking Gîtes
Beds in lodges should always be booked well ahead. Full board is generally obligatory.

3 Refuges
Refuge places are allocated on a first-come-first-served basis. Camping and bivouacking are permitted around the huts.

4 Waymarks
Do not venture away from the waymarks unless you have the navigation skills to find them again.

5 Water
Always check with the locals about water sources, and take along a spare bottle in case you run out.

6 Sun
Underestimate the power of the Corsican sun at your peril. Sunstroke at high altitude can be lethal.

7 Guide Books
The Féderation Française de la Randonnée Pédestre (FFRP) publishes excellent guides for all Corsica's long-distance routes (www.ffrandonnee.fr).

8 Hygiene
Dispose of toilet paper responsibly; do not leave it on the trails.

9 Trekking Poles
Carry a pair of adjustable trekking poles to ease the knee strain on long ascents and descents.

10 Fuel
If you plan to cook, take a multi-fuel stove, as not all makes of gas canister are available in Corsica.

≣10 Corsican Wildlife

① Corsican Deer
Based on the island for over 8,000 years, Corsican deer have evolved with shorter legs than other red deer. Although the last one was killed by a poacher in the 1960s, individuals of the same species have been successfully reintroduced from Sardinia into the Parc Naturel Régional de Corse *(see p107)*.

② Hermann's Tortoises
These tortoises with yellow-and-black patterned shells live in the maquis, but have become endangered on Corsica as a consequence of wildfires and road accidents. Visitors are welcome to visit the Parc Naturel Régional's breeding centre at the Village des Tortues de Moltifao *(see p62)*.

Hermann's tortoise in the maquis

③ Mouflons
Notable for their large, curling horns, Europe's only wild sheep were introduced from Anatolia in Neolithic times. Now the island's emblematic animal, they gave their Corsican name to the musical group I Muvrini. Look for them leaping fearlessly over steep ledges in the Parc Naturel Régional.

An impressively horned mouflon

④ Bearded Vultures (Lammergeiers)
Europe's largest native birds of prey stand 1.2 m (4 ft) high, with wingspans up to 2.7 m (9 ft). They nest on rocky ledges in Corsica's highest valleys. Some 80 per cent of their diet is bone marrow, obtained by dropping bones from a height.

Bearded vulture

⑤ Corsican Nuthatch (Sitelle)
France's only endemic bird, the 12-cm (5-in) blue-grey, black and white sitelle inhabits Corsica's Laricio pine forests and lives primarily on a diet of pine nuts. It has the curious habit of walking down tree trunks headfirst.

⑥ Golden Eagles
High mountain dwellers, golden eagles have been clocked diving for their prey (usually hares) at 200 km/h (125 mph). Corsican shepherds used to chant magic spells on Christmas Eve to keep them away from their lambs. There are some 30 nesting pairs in the Parc Naturel Régional.

⑦ Wild Boar
One of the island's most common beasts, boar often mate with wild pigs. They are quite shy, but if you meet a sow with piglets in the woods, you should walk quietly away. Boar cause a lot of damage to farms and vineyards – and they often appear on menus.

Corsican fire salamander

8 Corsican Fire Salamander

The island's native salamander owes its name to its bright yellow or orange markings. Because it needs moisture to survive and breeds in fresh water, look for it in deciduous forests at moderate altitudes near streams. You may find one hiding in a cool spot on a hot summer's day.

9 Ospreys (Sea Eagles)

The only large bird of prey to live exclusively off fish, the osprey is one of the big success stories of the Réserve Naturelle de Scandola (see p52). Reduced to four nesting pairs in 1970, today 32 of their messy seaweed-and-driftwood nests adorn the porphyry cliffs.

A pair of ospreys (sea eagles)

10 Corsican Donkey

Introduced by the Romans, this little donkey did the hard work on Corsica's steep terrain for centuries. It is now endangered, and there have been calls for it to be recognized as a separate species. Meanwhile, some have been finding new work, especially transporting baggage or children on treks.

TOP 10 CORSICAN PLANTS

1 Laricio Pines
Corsica's majestic native pines have distinctive pyramidal crowns and grow as high as 50 m (164 ft); the oldest are in the Forêt d'Aïtone (see p48).

2 Olive Trees
Introduced by the ancient Greeks, some trees in the Balagne are over 2,000 years old. Six varieties are made into Corsica's prized AOP olive oil.

3 Sweet Chestnut
Corsica's Castagniccia is the largest chestnut forest in Europe. The crop is made into flour and beer.

4 Fenouil
One of the strongest scents of the maquis comes from wild fennel, which is often used to flavour fish dishes.

5 Myrtle
This small tree is a symbol of love and immortality. Its dark-blue berries are used to make a liqueur.

6 Cistus (Rock Rose)
This plant's pink or white blooms add a note of colour to the maquis between March and July.

7 Asphodel
Asphodel's long stalks and white flowers were traditionally associated with the dead and magic.

8 Arbutus (Strawberry Tree)
Bees make a prized honey from this maquis shrub's white flowers. Its berries are made into jam and liqueur.

9 Sweet Broom
In late spring and early summer, broom covers Corsica's hillsides in dramatic yellow swathes and delicate perfume.

10 Cork Oak
One of the few trees able to regenerate their bark, cork oaks grow mostly in southern Corsica.

Corsican cork oak trees

🔟 Wild Swims

1 Plage de Guignu
MAP D3 ■ Refuge de Ghignu: 04955 91735; Open May–mid-Oct; www.agriate.org

A 5- to 6-hour walk from the nearest road on the Désert des Agriate coastal path brings you to this magical cove. Its turquoise waters lie beyond the reach of all but the most determined trekkers. The Refuge de Ghignu (The Paillers) provides basic lodging.

Cascade des Anglais

2 Cascade des Anglais
In the early 20th century, these beautiful waterfalls, high on the watershed near the railway station in Vizzavona, used to attract daytripping English aristocrats from Ajaccio – hence their name. Now they are firmly on the tourist trail, thanks to the pine forest and grandiose mountain scenery on all sides. Call in for a coffee at the delightfully old-fashioned Hotel Monte d'Oro (see p97).

3 Cala Genovese and Cala Francese
MAP F1

This pair of isolated coves is the jewel of Cap Corse's northern shoreline. Piles of seaweed sometimes mask their soft white sand, but the water is clear and the shallows are ideal for kids of all ages – though you'll probably have to carry young children most of the way from Macinaggio (see p26).

4 Plage d'Argent
MAP J6

Appreciate the silver sand and turquoise water of the Sartenais coast in solitude at this remote cove. It can be reached after a 30-minute drive down a rutted track, opposite the turning for the Palaggiu menhirs (see p19), followed by another 30-minute trek over the gravelly sand of Plage de Tralicetu.

5 Piscines Naturelles d'Aïtone
MAP C6

This classic picnic spot is nestled under vast Laricio pine trees just below the Col de Vergio (see p80). The roar of the falls is just as invigorating as the deep pools they flow into, and there are river-smoothed granite boulders to sprawl on after taking a dip.

Clear waters at the Cala di Tuara

9 Pont Génois, Asco
MAP D5

A humpbacked, 16th-century Genoese bridge spans the stretch where the normally turbulent Asco river flows calm and deep. Bring a face mask to see the trout that lurk in the river's green depths, and put on a pair of hiking shoes so you can explore the ancient path continuing up the mountain. Asco village lies 22 km (14 miles) west of Ponte Leccia on the D147.

6 Cala di Tuara
MAP A6

After an hour's hot hike through the maquis dividing Girolata from the Col de la Croix *(see p82)*, Cala di Tuara is a welcome sight. Few can resist the lure of its amazingly clear water, shimmering blue above a bed of grey granite pebbles. The cove slopes down quickly and offers some terrific deep-water snorkelling.

7 Pont de Muricciolu, Albertacce
MAP C6

This heavenly bathing spot high in the Vallée de Niolo, beside another secluded old Genoese bridge, is generally the exclusive preserve of hikers following the Mare a Mare Nord path *(see p56)*. You can walk to it in about 20 minutes from the D84 – look for the trail peeling north just after the crucifix on the outskirts of Albertacce village.

8 Lonca
MAP B6

Although a bit crowded at the height of summer, this popular bathing place in the secluded Lonca Valley deserves a detour from the nearby D124. Deep green pools froth with water surging over granite slabs, shaded beneath a canopy of Mediterranean oak and chestnut forest. The site lies an easy 5-minute walk from the road.

Fango river running through Tuarelli

10 Tuarelli
MAP B5

On the edge of this far-flung hamlet in Corsica's rugged northwest, the Fango river drains through smoothed boulders that shelter perfect natural pools to swim in when water levels are low during the summer. A huge wall of blood-red mountains – the "Grande Barrière" of Paglia Orba's north face – forms an enthralling backdrop as you splash about.

📟 Children's Attractions

1 Donkey Rides
MAP J5 ▪ Fior di Lezza; Vallee di l'Ortolu, Sartene ▪ Plage Cupabia: open Jun–Sep ▪ Vallee di l'Ortolu: open year round ▪ 06183 92303

The countryside of the Ortolo Valley and the sandy coastline of Cupabia beach are perfect for exploring on donkey back. Ride through oak forests via ancient, paved mule tracks to the mountain villages over the valley or enjoy sea-splashed rides on the beach.

The bichrome U Trinighellu

2 A Cupulatta
More than 3,000 animals and 170 species of tortoises, turtles and terrapins are at this reptile centre (see p80). Kids are encouraged to handle a few of them, and there are usually some cute newborns to amuse visitors.

Tortoise at A Cupulatta

3 Tramway de Balagne
MAP C4 ▪ 04953 28061 ▪ Four to six departures daily ▪ www.train-corse.com

The train line across the mountains is one of the great experiences Corsica has to offer, but the journey can be a little too long for children. An option is to take the tramway train between L'Île Rousse and Calvi, also known as U Trinighellu, which skirts some fine beaches, stopping at 20 stations.

4 Village des Tortues de Moltifao
MAP D5 ▪ Route d'Asco, Tizzarella, Moltifao ▪ 04954 78503 ▪ Open May–Sep: 9:30am–1pm & 2:30–7pm daily; or by appt for guided visits only ▪ Adm ▪ www.villagedestortues. wordpress.com

With Corsican tortoises becoming increasingly rare due to habitat destruction, the focus in this sanctuary, run by the National Park Authority, is on breeding endemic species for release into the wild.

5 Jardin des Abeilles
MAP J3 ▪ Ocana 20117 ▪ 04952 38388 ▪ Open Jun–Sep: 9am–7pm daily (from 10am Sat & Sun); Apr–May: 9am–noon & 2–6pm Mon–Fri (Oct: from 10am); boutique open all year; tours closed mid-Oct–mid-May ▪ Adm ▪ www.lejardindesabeilles.com

Corsican honey is out of this world – especially the variety made from

L'Île-Rousse
St-Florent
Calvi
Lozari
Lama
Borgo
Argentella
Muro
Moltifao
Galéria
Tuarelli
Francardo
Ponte Leccia
Calasima
Sermano
Golfe de Porto
Corte
Vico
Vizzavona
Vezzani
Cargèse
Arbori
Tiuccia
Tavera
Bastelica
Ajaccio
Travo
Porticcio
Zicavo
Fozzaninco
Solenzara
Verghia
Favone
Casalabriva
Aullène
Fautea
Golfe de Valinco
Grossa
Sartène
Porto-Vecchio
Tizzano
Figari
Santa Giulia
Bonifacio

0 km   20
0 miles   20

maquis or chestnut-flower pollen. Tours of this little bee garden just outside Ajaccio introduces the honey-making process, with glimpses into a glass-sided hive and demonstrations of extraction techniques.

6 Corsica Forest
MAP L3 ■ On the D268 near Solenzara ■ 06161 80058 ■ Open Jun–Sep: 9am–6pm ■ Adm ■ www.corsica-forest.com

Just inland from Solenzara, Corsica Forest has a very well-equipped adventure park and a challenging via ferrata facility around a massive cliff overlooking a bend in the river. As ever, a head for heights is needed. Canyoning is an optional add-on.

7 A Tyroliana
MAP L4 ■ Route de Taglio Rosso, Poggio del Pino 20144, Ste-Lucie-de-Porto-Vecchio ■ 04952 17804, 06120 20176 ■ Open Apr–Oct: 10am–7pm daily ■ Adm ■ www.atyroliana.com

A short drive inland from the coast around Porto-Vecchio, this riverside adventure park offers a mix of vertigo-inducing thrills in a shady pine forest, with pleasant picnic spots and river swimming nearby.

Colourful tri-yaks on the shore

8 Tri-yaking
MAP L5 ■ Sporsica: Pinarello (06242 65183) and Campomoro (06141 16882) ■ Mid-Apr–mid-Oct: 10am–7pm

Rent a tri-yak – just like a kayak, only with places for two adults and a child – for a paddle around the Pinarello bay and its adjacent island – ideal for beginners of sea canoeing.

Corsica Madness Adventure Park

9 Corsica Madness Adventure Park
MAP L4 ■ Bavella ■ 04957 86176, 06132 29506 ■ Open Apr–mid-Oct: 9:30am–6:30pm ■ Adm ■ www.corsicamadness.com

This sprawling adventure park, in a Laricio pine forest just below the Aiguilles de Bavella, occupies a most spectacular site. Choose between three circuits featuring monkey bridges, vertical nets and 110-m (360-ft) zip wires – all against wonderful mountain views.

10 Parc Naturel d'Olva
MAP J5 ■ Route de la Castagna, Sartène ■ 06117 52964 ■ Open Jun–Sep: 9:30am–7pm daily; Oct & Apr–May: 10am–6pm daily; Nov–Mar: 10am–6pm Wed–Sun (also Tue in school hols) ■ Adm ■ www.parc-animalier-corse.com

Children can mingle with a menagerie of donkeys, goats, ponies, ducks, chickens and peacocks at this small-holding in the Rizzanese Valley, just below Sartène. The farmers organize nature walks and goat-milking demonstrations. There's also a café and a picnic area as well.

Culinary Specialities

① Charcuterie

The diet of Corsica's free-range pigs – windfallen chestnuts, roots and wild berries – is the secret behind the island's aromatic cured meats. They come in a variety of forms: *prisutu* (ham); *lonzu* (fillet); *figatellu* (strong liver sausage); *coppa* (shoulder); *valetta* (cheek) and *salamu* (spicy salami).

Jars of *miel de châtaigne*

② Miel de Châtaigne (Chestnut Flower Honey)

If you like your honey strong and packed with exotic aromas, pick up a pot of *miel de châtaigne* at a local deli and prepare yourself for a taste of heaven. Chestnut-flour biscuits provide the ideal accompaniment.

③ Brocciu

Brocciu (pronounced "broodge") is soft ewe's cheese, produced uniquely in the winter. Corsicans love the full flavour and creamy texture it lends to many dishes. It blends wonderfully with mint for the filling in cannelloni and the stuffing for Bonifacio's traditional baked aubergine.

④ Veal and Olives

This classic Corsican dish features on the menus of most Corsican restaurants all year round. Like the pigs, local calves tend to be grazed in the maquis, where they feed on unfertilized woodland and mountain pastures, ensuring a fuller flavour which is perfectly complemented by strong Alta Rocca olives.

⑤ Tianu (Game Stew)

Corsicans are passionate hunters and will shoot anything that flutters in the maquis. Most of the small game ends up in hearty *tianu* (stew), typically made with *bécasse* (woodcock), *pédrix* (partridge), *caille* (quail) and other such birds.

⑥ Pietra Beer

Corsicans have always dried chestnuts to make flour, and in 1996 local couple Armelle and Dominique Sialelli found that it also made a superb amber beer. One of Corsica's economic success stories, the brewery in Furiani now produces different flavours and Corsica-Cola.

⑦ Sanglier (Wild Boar)

Despite the annual onslaught from hunters in the winter, wild boar remain prolific in the forests of the Corsican interior. If you're here during hunting season, you'll find local menus dominated by wild-pork stews and fillets, grilled with maquis herbs in smoky open hearths.

Sanglier (wild boar)

Slices of chestnut cake

8 Chestnuts

The Genoese planted whole forests of chestnut trees on the island, and the flour derived from the dried nuts is still an essential ingredient in many traditional dishes, particularly those of the mountains. Most patisseries in Corsica serve a range of cakes and pastries and even bread, made with chestnut flour.

Beignets (fritters)

9 Beignets (Fritters)

Light and nutty, chestnut-flour beignets are a perennial Corsican favourite, often served as a starter. The best are made with brocciu. Beignets are often wrongly translated on menus as "doughnuts", which does not do them justice.

10 Fromage de Brébis (Ewe's Cheese)

Pungent and filled with mountain flavours, Corsican matured ewe's cheese derives its intensity from the herb-filled pastures the sheep graze on during the summer, and the cheese-making techniques used by shepherds, which have altered little over the ages.

TOP 10 MARKETS AND DELIS

1 Open-Air Food Market, Ajaccio
A huge selection of locally produced charcuterie, cheese and wine (see p12).

2 L'Ef, Propriano
MAP J5 ▪ Vigna Majo ▪ 04952 51053 ▪ Open 9:30am–7pm Mon–Sat
Enjoy Corsican charcuterie, desserts and wine here.

3 Tempi Fa, Propriano
MAP J5 ▪ 7 Ave Napoleon ▪ 04957 60652
A deli selling superb terrines.

4 Bergerie d'Acciola, near Sartène
Cheese crêpes and bakes (see p89).

5 L'Orriu, Porto-Vecchio
MAP L5 ▪ 5 Cours Napoléon ▪ 04952 59589 ▪ Open Apr–Dec ▪ Closed some of Nov & Dec
Top-notch local charcuterie and mountain cheese. Has a wine bar.

6 Farmers' Market, Bastia
MAP P5 ▪ Place de l'Hôtel de Ville ▪ Open 7am–1pm Sat & Sun
The gastronomic heart of the city.

7 U Paese, Bastia
MAP P5 ▪ 4 Rue Napoléon ▪ Open 9am–noon, 3–7pm Mon–Sat
Fine charcuterie, cheese and wine from Castagniccia.

8 Marché Couvert, L'Île Rousse
MAP C4 ▪ Place Paoli ▪ Open 8am–1pm
A good variety of Corsican produce.

9 Annie Traiteur, Calvi
MAP B4 ▪ 5 Rue Clemenceau ▪ 04956 54967 ▪ Open Easter–Oct: 7:30am–8:30pm
Superb charcuterie hangs in this shop packed with Corsican produce.

10 U Stazzu, Ajaccio
MAP P2 ▪ 1, Rue Bonaparte ▪ 04955 11080 ▪ www.ustazza.com
The island's top charcuterie producers.

Charcuterie in U Stazzu, Ajaccio

🔟 Restaurants

Outdoor terrace overlooking the harbour at Le Pirate, Erbalunga

1 Le Pirate, Erbalunga

A Corsican institution, this Michelin-starred restaurant (see p103) offers a creative menu. Try lobster tortellini with shellfish cream and sprinklings of roasted hazelnuts, or the fragrant octopus risotto, simmered in squid ink. Book well in advance.

2 Casadelmar, Porto-Vecchio

The setting, overlooking the bay, is stunning, the decor is chic, and chef Fabio Bragagnolo has two Michelin stars (see p112). Dishes such as cuttlefish and lobster lasagne combine Corsican and Italian traditions.

3 Le Grand Oggi, Lumio

On a stylish terrace looking across the gulf of Calvi, Le Grand Oggi (see p103) is a Michelin-starred restaurant in the Hôtel Chez Charles, which serves modern cuisine with a strong French-Corsican accent. It offers four differently priced fixed menus, including one with exotic flavours from around the world.

4 Ferme-Auberge Campo di Monte, Murato

Travelling to this farmhouse (see p103), in the Nebbio hills above St-Florent, is an adventure in itself, and Madame Juillard's traditional cooking – veal in olives, river trout stuffed with *brocciu* and *beignets* – doesn't disappoint. Ask for a table on the terrace, with spectacular views of the gulf.

5 Monte d'Oro

With a view of the mountain bearing its name, this celebrated ivy-covered restaurant (see p97) has a 19th-century feel to it. The specialties served here include duck, veal and Corsican desserts. Treat yourself to a room in their charming hotel.

6 A Pignata, Alta Rocca

Fabulous local cuisine is served in this idyllic rural setting (see p89). If it is on the menu, go for the perfect slow-roasted lamb with *cannelloni au brocciu*.

Interior of A Pignata, Alta Rocca

7 La Roya, St-Florent
The seafood is cooked to perfection, the chocolate desserts are divine and the tasting menu is highly recommended at Michelin-starred La Roya *(see p103)*. The idyllic setting – in a garden with views of the sea and the setting sun – adds to the magic.

8 A Nepita, Ajaccio
This Michelin-starred restaurant *(see p83)* is one place you can be assured of fine cooking. The menu changes daily and features exquisite dishes created from the best seasonal ingredients from the local market. There is also an excellent wine list.

Chic L'Altru Versu, Ajaccio

9 L'Altru Versu, Ajaccio
This is Corsican fine dining that relies on its ingredients *(see p83)*. Signature dishes include fish from the gulf baked with *brocciu* and clementine oil, veal with mushrooms and lemon and *brocciu* tart with mountain thyme and saffron sorbet. Reservations are essential.

10 Le Bélvèdere, Côti-Chiavari
Typical Corsican home-style cooking, with dishes such as grilled wild boar and chestnut-flour polenta, is served on a terrace with a phenomenal view of the entire gulf of Ajaccio and its mountainous hinterland *(see p83)*. Moreover, eating here can be relatively economical, though you will need to reserve well in advance.

TOP 10 SPOTS FOR AN APÉRITIF

Place de la République

1 Place de la République, Porto-Vecchio
MAP L5
A Genoese square where Italians show off their tans and designer clothes.

2 Place St-Nicholas, Bastia
MAP F3
The social hub of Bastia, this square is lined with terrace cafés.

3 Place des Portes, St-Florent
MAP E3
Watch the world go by over a glass of local muscat wine in this square.

4 Place Porta, Sartène
MAP J5
Ancient stone square where the town's social life is played out.

5 Place Gaffori, Corte
MAP D6
A great space to linger over a coffee in Corte's crumbling Genoese old town.

6 Quai Landry, Calvi
MAP B4
Calvi at its swankiest – Côte d'Azur panache with a Corsican backdrop.

7 Le Refuge, Cartalavonu
MAP K5 ▪ Massif de l'Ospédale ▪ 04957 00039 ▪ Closed Nov–Mar ▪ www.lerefuge-cartalavonu.com
Experience the atmosphere of south Corsica's high pine forest at this lodge.

8 Auberge du Col de Bavella
Enjoy the view of the Bavella needles on the sunny terrace here *(see p89)*.

9 Le Chalet, Haut-Asco
MAP C5 ▪ Haut-Asco ▪ 04954 78108 ▪ Open noon–2:30pm, 7:30–10pm ▪ www.hotel-lechalet-asco.com
Admire the mighty Monte Cinto over an ice-cold Pietra beer at this ski resort.

10 Da Passano, Bonifacio
MAP K7 ▪ 53 Quai Jérôme Comparetti ▪ 04952 81090 ▪ Open 10:30am–4pm, 6:30pm–2am ▪ www.da-passano.com
Deli and wine bar on the port, with live guitar music on summer evenings.

🔟 Wineries

① Clos d'Alzeto

MAP H2 ▪ Sari d'Orcino, near Ajaccio ▪ 04955 22467 ▪ Open 8am–noon & 2–6pm Mon–Sat; Summer: 8am–12:30pm & 1:30–6:30pm Mon–Fri (from 9:30am Sat) ▪ www.closdalzeto.com

In a setting 500 m (1,640 ft) above sea level, Corsica's highest vineyards have been tended by the Albertini family since 1800. The unique microclimate yields fine, original wines: a spicy Sciaccurellu red, a clean, fruity Vermentinu and an exceptional rosé.

② Domaine Fiumicicoli

MAP J5 ▪ Rte de Levie, Sartène ▪ 04957 71020 ▪ Open Apr–Oct: 9am–noon & 2–6pm Mon–Fri ▪ www.domaine-fiumicicoli.com

Aged in American oak barrels, the red cuvée, Vassilia, is the flagship wine, but of equal pride are the herb-tinged white and red muscat dessert wines.

③ Domaine Gentile

MAP E3 ▪ Olzo, near St-Florent ▪ 04953 70154/72020 ▪ Visits by appt only

Classic Corsican wines, including one of the island's top muscats, are produced by hand according to strict organic principles in this region. The well-drained chalk-schist soil and optimum climate are perfect for wine-making, and the wines themselves are magnificent.

Barrels of wine in the Domaine Leccia

④ Domaine Leccia

MAP E3 ▪ Poggio d'Oletta, Morta-Piana, near St-Florent ▪ 04953 71135 ▪ Open 9am–7pm Mon–Sat, 10am–6pm Sun ▪ www.domaine-leccia.com

Corsican grape varieties Niellucciu (for reds) and Verminto (for whites) combine beautifully with the *terroir* of this third-generation vineyard in the hills outside St-Florent. State-of-the-art production complements a traditional growing style to produce award-winning vintages.

⑤ Domaine Antoine Arena

MAP E3 ▪ Morta Maio, D81, Patrimonio ▪ 04953 70827 ▪ Visits by appt only

Known as a "godfather" of Corsican wine, Arena produces a wine that is truly sublime – an expression of Corsican viticulture, identity and family values. Handed down for generations, the growing techniques have not changed over the years, and neither have the wines.

Vineyard at Clos Nicrosi

distinction. Pick up a bottle of the vineyard's benchmark "Oriu", considered one of Corsica's finest red.

⑥ Clos Nicrosi

MAP E1 ■ Rogliano, Macinaggio, Cap Corse ■ 04953 54117 ■ Open May–Sep: 10am–noon, 4–7pm Mon–Sat

This 25-acre vineyard in northern Cap Corse retains a distinctly Genoese overtone. The characterful wines it produces are much sought-after, but notoriously difficult to find unless you travel to Macinaggio yourself. Their white and muscat have a serious following among local wine buffs.

⑦ Domaine de Torraccia

MAP L5 ■ Lecci, near Porto-Vecchio ■ 04957 14350 ■ Open 8am–noon, 2–6pm (Jul & Aug: 8am–8pm) ■ www.domaine-de-torraccia.com

Christian Imbert was among the first to recognize the potential of Corsica's traditional vine stock and granitic soil in the 1960s. Grown organically, his hand-harvested grapes produce wines of great

⑧ Domaine Pieretti

MAP E2 ■ Santa Severa, Luri, Cap Corse ■ 04953 50103, 06179 39217 ■ Open Apr–Oct, or by appt only ■ www.vinpieretti.com

Lina Pieretti became the family's fifth-generation wine-maker in the late 1980s. The wines now produced owe their uniqueness to the unusual mix of Alicante and Niellucciu grapes, which thrive in the cape's dry, windy climate. Look out for the award-winning orange-scented muscat.

⑨ Clos Culombu

MAP B4 ■ Chemin San Pedru, Lumio, near Calvi ■ 04956 07068 ■ Open May–Oct: 9am–7pm Mon–Sat, 10am–1pm & 3–7pm Sun; Nov–Apr: 9am–noon & 1:30–6pm Mon–Sat or by appt only ■ www.closculombu.fr

On the outskirts of Lumio (see p31), Etienne Suzzoni's organic vineyards tend towards quality over quantity. The aromatic wines have a strong Corsican character. Enjoy the pink-grey rosé with local snapper; the red comes oaked as "Clos Cuvée" or the more traditional "Domaine".

⑩ Domaine Saparale

Saparale (see pp18–19) is buried deep in one of the wildest corners of the Sartenais. You can taste the crisp minerals of the Vallée de l'Ortolo in Philipe Farinelli's light-bodied wines. Their rosé garners rave reviews.

Domaine Saparale

🔟 Festivals

Holy Week celebrations as part of La Granitola, Calvi

1 La Granitola, Calvi
Good Friday

Calvi's Easter begins at 9pm on Good Friday, when penitents carry wooden crosses through the *basse ville* (lower town) to the cathedral square up.

2 La Cerca, Erbalunga
Good Friday

This Easter procession by masked brotherhoods begins at the church of St-Erasme on the outskirts of Erbalunga in Cap Corse.

3 U Catenacciu, Sartène
Good Friday

This procession of penitents draws its participants from *confraternità* (religious brotherhoods). Secrecy surrounds the identity of the red-robed Pénitent Rouge – a role often taken by repentant mafia godfathers.

U Catenacciu, Sartène

4 BD à Bastia
04953 21281 ▪ Late Mar/early Apr ▪ www.una-volta.org

The heart of Bastia's cartoon festival is an exhibition featuring an array of modern graphic art books, from time-honoured favourites such as Tintin to Marvel and anime.

5 Procession du Christ Noir, Bastia
3 May

The streets of Bastia's Citadelle form the backdrop for this religious procession, in which a black crucifix is paraded on the shoulders of devotees. The cross was discovered floating in the sea in 1428.

6 Rencontres Internationales de Théâtre en Corse, Olmi-Cappella, Pioggiola
04956 19318 ▪ Mid-Jul–mid-Aug ▪ www.ariacorse.org

This remote village in the Giunssani region transforms into the venue for a drama festival. Villagers perform plays on open-air stages and inter-nationally famous directors help the participants prepare.

7 Festival du Film du Lama
04954 82160 ▪ Late Jul/early Aug ▪ www.festilama.org

This niche film festival attracts film professionals from across Europe

and features movies inspired by
rural themes. Screenings take
place in an open-air cinema on the
outskirts of Lama (see p102), where
bourgeois houses stand in striking
contrast to the surrounding barren
mountain slopes.

8 Fêtes Napoléoniennes, Ajaccio
04955 15303 ■ Mid-Aug

Marching soldiers in First Empire
uniform and sound-and-light extrav-
aganzas bring a splash of pageantry
to the Corsican capital in August,
when the town celebrates the
birthday of its most illustrious
son. The grand finale, featuring an
ear-splitting display of fireworks,
is on Ascension Day (15 Aug).

9 A Santa di u Niolu
Vallée de Niolo ■ 04954
80331 ■ Sep

This age-old festival sees the
bars in the mountain village
of Casamaccioli overflow with
aficionados of a dying Corsican
art form – *chama i rispondi*. The
performers improvise insults in
rhyming couplets.

A Santa di u Niolu

10 Festival International du Cirque de Corse, Bastia and Ajaccio
04955 14722 ■ Oct ■ www.imperial
show.com

Circus troupes from across the
globe compete in this spectacular
celebration, with exotic animals,
jugglers, trainers and trapeze artists.

TOP 10 COUNTRY FAIRS

Cheeses at A Fiera di u Casgiu

1 Les Agrumes en Fête, Bastelicaccia
www.fetedesagrumes.com ■ Feb
Exhibitors display citrus produce; some
recipes date from the Court of Louis XV.

2 Festa di L'Oliu Novu, Sainte Lucie de Tallano
06212 92418 ■ Apr
Corsicans welcome spring by
celebrating their hearty olive oil.

3 A Fiera di u Casgiu, Venaco
04954 71519 ■ May
The smell of cheese permeates the air
at the island's largest cheese festival.

4 Pescadori in Festa, Ajaccio
Early Jun
Fishermen (and seafood) are the focus
of five days of feasting and activities.

5 Fiera di u Vinu, Luri
04953 50644 ■ Jul
Sample Corsica's finest wines in an
inspiring setting on Cap Corse.

6 Fiera di l'Avilu, Montegrosso
04956 28172 ■ Jul
This fair in the Balagne mountains is
dedicated to Corsican olive production.

7 Foire de l'Amandier, Aregno
06195 62489 ■ Aug
A fair to promote Corsica's ailing
almond industry.

8 Festa di u Ficu, Peri
www.festadiuficu.com ■ Sep
A long-standing celebration of the
regions' fig production and specialities.

9 U Mele in Fiesta, Murzu
Late Sep
Murzo, north of Ajaccio, celebrates
honey from the maquis with a fair.

10 Fiera di a Castagna, Bocognano
www.fieradiacastagna.com ■ Dec
Food producers from all over the island
present chestnut products.

TOP10 Music Festivals

Performance at Les Nuits de la Guitare, Patrimonio

1 Jazz in Ajaccio
04955 15303/14544,
0623239213 ■ Late Jun ■ www.jazz
inaiacciu.com

This annual festival brings together
big-name artists for a performance
under the stars. It headlines
everything from jazz and blues to
modern and instrumental music.

2 Festivoce, Balagne
04956 17313 ■ Mid-Jul
■ www.centreculturelvoce.org

Corsican vocal music forms the basis
of this lively festival in Balagne. The
larger events are staged in Pigna's
modern, Moorish-style theatre.
Free sunset serenades take place
every evening of the festival.

3 Calvi on the Rocks
Mid-Jul ■ www.calvion
therocks.com

While not a big festival by international
standards, this is great fun nonethe-
less. It is held at the height of summer,
and bands and DJs play on open-air
stages behind the beach.

Crowds gather at Calvi on the Rocks

4 Les Nuits de la Guitare, Patrimonio
04953 71215 ■ Jul ■ www.festival-
guitare-patrimonio.com

This guitar festival, held in the square
below the village's church, has seen
an impressive line-up of stars such
as John McLaughlin, Elvis Costello,
Gilberto Gil, Patti Smith and the great
flamenco artist Tomatito. Django
Reinhardt-style gypsy jazz tends to
wrap up the event.

5 Festival di Musica Classica, Santa Reparata di Balagna
06454 00026 ■ Early Aug ■ www.
musica-classica.fr

For three nights in August, one of the
Balagne's prettiest villages provides a
romantic outdoor setting for classical
music recitals by singers, chamber
music groups and classical guitarists.
Conferences on music take place
before the concerts.

6 Porto Latino, St-Florent
Aug ■ www.portolatino.fr

For four nights, St-Florent's Place des
Portes resounds to salsa, mambo and
Brazilian cumbia, as top-draw Latin
dance groups take to the stage in this
music festival.

7 Festival de Musique d'Erbalunga
06093 25534 ■ Aug ■ www.
festivaldemusiqueerbalunga.com

A floodlit Genoese watchtower at the
entrance to Erbalunga's tiny harbour

provides a backdrop for this high-season festival, held in the village's little square. French jazz and "le Rock" dominate proceedings over the long weekend in August.

⑧ U Settembrinu, Tavagna
Eastern Corsica ▪ 04953 69194, 06224 98128 ▪ **Late Aug**

This week-long event transforms the local squares into lively open-air stages in the Tavagna region. Rock, world music and folk are its mainstay with a strong showing from Corsican polyphony fusion artists.

Rencontres de Chants Polyphoniques

⑨ Rencontres de Chants Polyphoniques, Calvi and Bastia
04956 52357 ▪ **Mid-Sep**

Corsica's most famous polyphonic choir, A Filetta, presides over this annual festival, which attracts artists from all over the world. Mongolian throat singers, Bulgarian women's choirs and Georgian monks have all appeared in the past.

⑩ Les Musicales de Bastia
04953 27591 ▪ **Nov**
▪ www.musicales-de-bastia.com

Mostly French and Italian stars perform at Corsica's oldest and last big music festival of the year. Performances take place over five nights at different venues in Bastia, ranging from the Second Empire theatre to the Oratoire Ste-Croix.

TOP 10 CORSICAN POLYPHONY ALBUMS

I Muvrini on stage

1 *A Bercy*, **I Muvrini**
This is a platinum-selling live album of I Muvrini's performance at Bercy, Paris.

2 *Per Agata*, **Donnisulana**
An all-women ensemble's debut album, which took the Corsican music world by storm.

3 *Corsica Sacra*, **Jacky Micaelli**
The finest female voice of her generation, Jacky is most expressive in this sparse, passionate recording.

4 *Intantu*, **A Filetta**
The island's foremost group is renowned for its traditional and contemporary polyphony.

5 *A Cappella*, **Tavagna**
An old-school quintet from the island's eastern interior singing sublime polyphony.

6 *Polyphonies*, **Voce di Corsica**
A "supergroup" of Corsican singers formed in the 1990s. This album of polphony ranks as among the island's most popular.

7 *L'Âme Corse*, **Various Artists**
An album showcasing Corsica's polyphony output, with some instrumental tracks.

8 *U Cantu di e Donne*, **Isulatine**
A mixture of original compositions and traditional songs by an all-women group.

9 *Isulanima*, **Trio Soledonna**
Traditional musicians from around the Mediterranean team up with three of Corsica's finest female singers.

10 *Poletti et le Choeur d'Hommes de Sartène*
Traditional polyphony performed by the legend Jean-Paul Poletti and his male-voice choir group.

Corsica
Area by Area

Boats moored in Vieux Port, Bastia

Ajaccio and the West Coast

Ajaccio, Corsica's flamboyant capital, has two distinct facets: the touristy imperial city, with its pastel-washed alleyways and pretty fishing harbour, and the suburbs of tower blocks spilling over the surrounding hills. The two inhabit largely separate worlds. Few visitors stray further from the waterfront than the 18th-century streets of the old quarter, where Napoleon grew up. The Maison Bonaparte and the Palais Fesch, with its collection of Renaissance and Baroque art, are the two principal sights, both easily reached in a day trip from the resorts on the gulf's southern shore. Further north, the landscape grows increasingly spectacular as you approach the Golfe de Porto, whose orange cliffs are the scenic highlight of the west coast.

Statue of Napoleon Bonaparte

AJACCIO AND THE WEST COAST

Marseille, Genoa, Nice, Toulon

Réserve Naturelle de Scandola
Partinello
Golfe de Porto
Capo Rosso
Piana
Ota
Plage d'Arone
Spelunca Gorge
Revinda
Plage de Pero
Cargèse
Sagone
Arbori
Vico
Arro
Tiuccia
Golfe de Sagone
Appietto
Golfe de Lava
Capo di Feno
Alata
Ajaccio
Porticcio
Golfe d'Ajaccio
Plage de Verghia
Portigliolo
Verghia
Cala d'Orzu
Porto, Torres

Calasima Calacuccia
Albertacce
Lonca
Evisa
Lac de Nino Lac de Capitello
GR20
Marignana
Renno Soccia
Guagno-les-Bains Guagno
Rezza
Ambiegna
Vallée de la Gravona
Liscia
Peri Tavera
Ucciani
Carbuccia
Tolla
THE MICHELINE
Eccica-Suarella
Campo dell'Oro
Cauro
Ste-Marie-Siche
Côti-Chiavari
Petreto-Bicchisano
Tavaro

Mediterranean Sea

Top 10 Sights
see pp77–9

Restaurants
see p83

The Best of the Rest
see p80

Interior Villages
see p81

Day Walks
see p82

0 kilometres   10
0 miles   10

The fishing harbour at Ajaccio

1 Ajaccio

A winter livestock market in Roman times, Ajaccio *(see pp12–13)* became a major settlement only after the Genoese erected a citadel here in the late 15th century. It expanded rapidly from 1580, and by the mid-17th century had become Corsica's foremost port. Today, it serves as Corsica's main tourist gateway. Above all else, it is famous as being the birthplace of Napoleon, a connection underlined by statues of the "Little Corporal" dominating the town's squares.

2 Plage de Verghia
MAP H4

In Côti-Chiavari, at the very end of the bus route from Ajaccio, this is the least frequented of the sandy bays along the Rive Sud and by far the prettiest. Shallow, crystal-clear water and powdery white sand make it a perfect choice for young families. Pine trees crowning the headland to the west provide shade, and one of the island's more welcoming beach cafés, La Plage d'Argent, serves cold beers on the dune behind.

3 Cala d'Orzu
MAP H4

After the manicured beaches of the Rive Sud, Cala d'Orzu offers a distinct change of tone. The atmosphere here is ruled by the churning waves of nearby Capo di Muro *(see p82)*, where a lighthouse surveys a shoreline that feels a million miles away from wthe Riviera chic of Ajaccio. The bay and its adjacent coves are great for snorkelling and are deserted most weekdays.

4 Cargèse
MAP G1 ■ www.cargese.net

In the 17th century, some 730 refugees from a bloody vendetta in the southern Peloponnese alighted on Corsica's west coast near Cargèse. Four hundred years on, their descendents are still here, living in a cluster of neat stone houses set around the village's two churches – one Latin Catholic, one Greek Orthodox. The Greek church, St-Spyridon, holds original icons brought from Mani in 1676, including a 12th-century painting of the Virgin and Child.

Church of St-Spyridon, Cargèse

5 Plage de Pero
MAP G1

Backed by a scattering of hotels and holiday villas, this well-sheltered bay north of Cargèse makes a great pit stop on long journeys up the west coast. After a dip in its transparent water, stretch your legs with a walk to a 17th-century Genoese watch-tower perched on the tip of the headland to the north. Fine views from the tower extend up the coast.

The rooftops of Piana, surrounded by the Calanche rocks

6 Spelunca Gorge
MAP B7

The cliffs of the Spelunca Gorge reach a height of 1000 m (3,280 ft), soaring above a wild valley carpeted in forest and maquis. You can enjoy the landscape by following the old paved trails winding through the gorge, or from the depths of a pool in the river on the valley floor.

Dramatic cliffs of the Spelunca Gorge

7 Golfe de Porto

The west coast's prime visitor attraction, the Golfe de Porto (see pp34–5) is unique in the Mediterranean for its red porphyry landscapes. The views extending across the sapphire waters of the bay to the molten-red headlands of Capo Rosso and Scandola are unforgettable. Edward Lear, who travelled through the area in 1868, was amazed by its grandeur, rendering the scenery in a series of line drawings.

8 Piana
MAP A7

Piana (see p35) has served as the principal springboard for tours to the nearby Calanche rocks since long before the Corniche was surfaced. Its flower-filled 17th-century square continues to attract a steady stream of visitors during the summer months. Although there is nothing much to do here beyond penning a postcard or two on a sunny café terrace, explorations of the village's cacti-covered fringes reveal spellbinding vistas of the gulf. If you are here at Easter, do not miss the Granitola procession of hooded penitents, starting at the picturesque Ste-Pierre-et-Paul church.

9 Plage d'Arone
MAP A7

This heavenly beach lies at the foot of a sweep of deserted mountains below Piana and can be reached via the D824. Swimming in turquoise water amid such imposing scenery is an experience that is hard to beat. There is very little else nearby except for a campsite and a few pleasant café-restaurants where you can snack while looking out over the beach. The path winding through the maquis from the north side of the bay leads to a rocky headland, where you can enjoy magnificent views north to Capo Rosso.

GENOESE BRIDGES

A typical feature of Corsica's rural landscape are the Genoese bridges over many of its rivers **(below)**. Although some of these steeply sloping, single-span structures were built in the 1200s, most of them date from the 15th and 16th centuries, when the booming trade in chestnut flower, timber and wine required year-round crossing points.

10 Capo Rosso
MAP A7

The most southerly of the Herculean red promontories standing guard at the mouth of the Golfe de Porto, Capo Rosso forms a classic humpback shape, its red cliffs rising vertically from the waves to a solitary Genoese watchtower (see p46). The panoramic views from the top are unbelievably beautiful, but it is a long, steep climb. Taking around 3 hours to walk to the top and back, the path starts 7 km (4 miles) west of Piana on the D824.

Ancient tower on Capo Rosso

A WALK AROUND AJACCIO

▶ MORNING

Kick-start your day's sightseeing at one of the workers' cafés fronting the César Campinchi square. From there, follow the narrow backstreet behind the square on to the Rue Fesch, site of the famous **Palais Fesch** (see pp14–15). You will need a good couple of hours to work your way around its highlights. Retracing your steps back down the rue Fesch, emerge at the palm-lined Place Foch. Napoleon aficionados will love the memorabilia in the **Salon Napoléonien** (see p13), which is a short walk from the Emperor's birthplace, the **Maison Bonaparte** (see p13), where you can see the divan on which he was born. Nearby, the **U Stazzu** deli (see p65) is one of the city's best Corsican-produce shops, selling fine charcuterie, wines and honey.

AFTERNOON

Pause for lunch at one of the quayside restaurants on the Port Tino Rossi, then follow the road skirting the Genoese **Citadelle** (see p13) and St François beach until you see the **Ajaccio Cathedral** (see p12) on your right, worth a visit for its evocative Delacroix painting inside the doorway. A short walk from there across the Place de Gaulle, dominated by a statue of Napoleon and his brothers, brings you to Ajaccio's main shopping street, Cours Napoléon, where **Grand Café Napoléon** (see p83) provides a haven from the mêlée of the town centre.

See map on p76 ⬅

The Best of the Rest

 A Cupulatta
MAP J2 ▪ Vignola, Vero, Ucciani, 17 km northeast of Ajaccio ▪ 04955 28234 ▪ Open Apr–mid-May & mid-Sep–mid-Nov: 10am–5:30pm; mid-May–mid-Sep 9am–7pm ▪ Adm ▪ www.acupulatta.com

This sanctuary is home to a great collection of tortoises and other reptiles, from Jurassic-looking giants to teeny terrapins. It is 30 minutes northeast of Ajaccio on the N193.

 Porticcio
MAP H3

The largest of the Rive Sud's ribbon of resorts, Porticcio is centred on a broad, sandy beach. Take a bus from Ajaccio or a boat from the old port.

③ Portigliolo
MAP H4

This idyllic, semi-circular bay at the southwestern extremity of the Golfe d'Ajaccio has a laid-back beach and a well-sheltered snorkelling spot.

④ Golfe de Sagone
MAP G2

Dip your toes in the water of this spectacular beach at Sagone, the next gulf up the coast from Ajaccio.

 Plage de Bussaglia
MAP A6

If you are in the Porto area and keen to avoid the crowds, this curve of grey pebbles and blue water, cradled by steep promontories, is the best option.

The elegant Plage de Bussaglia

Scenic Col de Vergio

 Col de Vergio
MAP C6

For a taste of dramatic forests and mountains, head up to the rock-strewn "Pass of the Virgin", dividing the Spelunca and Niolo gorges at the nexus of two major footpaths.

 Le Bélvèdere, Forêt d'Aïtone
MAP C7

This natural balcony formed by boulders at the head of the Spelunca Gorge is a great starting point for walks through the Forêt d'Aïtone.

 Plage de Chiuni
MAP A7

An amazingly secluded bay, Chiuni has a small Club Med complex but little else to mar its pristine setting.

 Plage de Gradelle
MAP A6

Sublime sunset views across the gulf to Capo d'Orto and the Calanche are the chief asset of this beach (see p35), northwest of the Golfe de Porto.

⑩ Pont de Zaglia
MAP B7

This Genoese bridge, inland from Porto, is where walkers following the trail from Evisa to Ota (see p56) come for a spot of swimming.

Interior Villages

Vico
MAP H1

To escape the tourist trail completely, head 15 km (9 miles) inland from Sagone to Vico, where the medieval, café-lined square offers plenty of shade and a peaceful atmosphere.

Tolla
MAP J2

For a total change of vibe from Ajaccio, head east up the Gorges du Prunelli to Tolla, a sleepy granite village overlooking a huge spread of lake and craggy mountains.

Marignana
MAP B7

Marignana's pretty cluster of red-tiled houses with old stone balconies jutting over the chestnut canopy comes as a heavenly vision for walkers on this region's trails.

Soccia
MAP C7

The tarmac comes to an end at Soccia, a breathtaking mountain village from where ancient mule tracks, now used by walkers, lead to the surrounding ridges and forests.

Renno
MAP C7

A bastion of traditional Corsican hill culture, Renno is one of the island's remotest settlements. Each February, the annual mass pig slaughter provides an excuse for a popular rural fair, A Tumbera.

Revinda
MAP B7

Corsica's smallest permanently inhabited village is on a lonely hillside above Cargèse (see p77). Aside from the views, the main attraction is nearby refuge E Case (see p117).

Guagno-les-Bains
MAP J1

Pascal Paoli was among the patrons of this spa in the Sagone hinterland, whose thermal, sulphurous waters remain a sought-after cure for rheumatic and skin disorders.

Evisa
MAP B7

Chestnut trees and the age-old traditions of pig rearing govern life in this picturesque hill village above the Spelunca Gorge – popular as much for its cuisine as its forest walks.

The pretty village of Evisa

Ota
MAP B7

Clinging to a steep, maquis-covered hillside above Porto, this classic mountain village of 17th-century granite houses boasts stupendous views across the valley to the north cliffs of Capo d'Orto (see p35).

Côti-Chiavari
MAP H4

An unforgettable panorama of sea and mountains unfolds from Côti-Chiavari. Its pale-grey houses, reached via a tortuous series of switchbacks from the Rive Sud, straddle high above the Golfe d'Ajaccio.

See map on p76 ←

Day Walks

 Capo d'Orto
MAP B7

An immense 360-degree panorama over Corsica's most sublime landscape is the reward for ascending Capo d'Orto (see p35), the sugarloaf summit looming above Porto. The trail starts 1.5 km (1 mile) east of Piana.

Views from Capo d'Orto

 Ota to Serriera
MAP B6

One of the benchmark stages of the Tra Mare e Monti Nord trail (see p57), this route winds over the 900-m- (2,950-ft-) high San Petru pass. Enjoy the marvellous panorama over the Golfe de Porto.

 Evisa to Marignana
MAP B7

This leisurely amble through the leafy woodland separating two of the island's loveliest villages makes for an ideal day-long walk. Stop for lunch at Ustaria di a Rota (see p117).

4 Col de Vergio to Cascades de Radule
MAP C6

An immensely enjoyable hike over the sun-drenched, rocky terrain of the upper Golo Valley brings you to a blue-green pool fed by a perennial waterfall. This is a lovely spot to swim in the water and sunbathe.

5 Col de la Croix to Girolata
MAP A6

This classic Corsican 3-hour hike takes you from the Golfe de Porto's Corniche to the coastal village of Girolata (see p35), via hillsides of dense maquis and a beautiful cove.

6 Château Fort
MAP B7

A colossal chunk of red porphyry that resembles a castle, the Château Fort marks the end point of a varied, hour-long jaunt north of the Roches Bleues café, through the Calanche rock formations.

7 Sentier Muletier
MAP B7

A small oratory in the cliff, 500 m (1,640 ft) south of the Roches Bleues café, flags the head of this tougher trail through the Calanche via the path that connects Ota and Piana.

8 Evisa to Pont de Zaglia
MAP B7

Follow a zigzagging medieval track, with original cobbles intact, through chestnut and oak forest to this Genoese packhorse bridge (see p80), where you can bathe in the river.

9 Chemin des Crêtes
MAP H3

A superb ridge route, the Chemin des Crêtes heads uphill from Ajaccio, following the rocky spine of the mountain that rises behind the city.

10 Capo di Muro
MAP H4

This is the nearest stretch of wild coast if you track the shoreline south from Ajaccio. An old watchtower makes the perfect target for a walk along the headland (see pp46–7).

Restaurants

1 **Grand Café Napoléon**
MAP P2 ■ 10–12 Cours Napoléon, Ajaccio ■ 04952 14254 ■ Closed Sun ■ €€€
Dine in the tearoom, or in the opulent Second Empire restaurant in Ajaccio's most elegant meeting place.

2 **A Nepita**
MAP H3 ■ 4 Rue San Lazaro, Ajaccio ■ 04952 67568 ■ Open Mon–Fri L, Thu–Sat D ■ €€€
The modern menu changes daily and features local fish and meat, plus excellent wines (see p67). Book ahead.

3 **Le 20123**
MAP P3 ■ 2 Rue du Roi de Rome, Ajaccio ■ 04952 15005 ■ Open D only ■ Closed Mon (winter) ■ €€
The tiny hamlet of Pina Canale (postcode 20123) has been re-created in central Ajaccio. Guests can collect their water from the village fountain and dine on authentic rural cuisine.

4 **Les Roches Rouges**
MAP A7 ■ Piana, Golfe de Porto ■ 04952 78181 ■ Open Mar–Nov ■ €€€
Gourmet cuisine is served in a frescoed *fin-de-siècle* dining hall with sublime views.

Interior of Les Roches Rouges

5 **Le Bélvèdere**
MAP H4 ■ Côti-Chiavari ■ 04952 71032 ■ Open Mar–mid-Nov: 7:30–9pm daily; Mar–May: Sun L ■ €€
Set in a bed-and-breakfast, high above the Rive Sud, this restaurant has fantastic views from its terrace.

PRICE CATEGORIES
For a three-course meal for one with half a bottle of wine (or equivalent meal), taxes and extra charges.

€ under €30   €€ €30–€50   €€€ over €50

6 **L'Altru Versu**
MAP H3 ■ Les Sept Chapelles, Route des Sanguinaires, Ajaccio ■ 04955 00522 ■ Open noon–8pm Thu–Mon ■ Closed winter (hours vary, call to check) ■ €€€
This restaurant (see p67), offering a refined, gourmet take on traditional Corsican mountain cuisine, is the first choice for foodies in the capital.

7 **A Casa Corsa, Piana**
MAP A7 ■ Route de Porto, Piana ■ 04952 45793 ■ Open 7am–midnight ■ €€
Choose your own lobster at this fresh seafood restaurant offering sunset views of the Calanche de Piana.

8 **L'Arbousier**
MAP H3 ■ Le Maquis, Porticcio ■ 04952 52015 ■ Open noon–2pm, 8–10pm ■ Closed mid-Jan–Feb ■ €€€
High Gallic gastronomy, made from local ingredients by chef Gérard Lorenzini, is served here on a terrace overlooking a private beach.

9 **A Tramula (Bar de la Poste)**
MAP B7 ■ Evisa ■ 04952 62439 ■ Open year round (Oct–mid-Apr by reservation only) ■ €€€
Relish the charcuterie, veal and other mountain delights on offer here. Ask for a table on the balcony.

10 **A Merendella Citadina**
MAP P3 ■ 19 Rue Conventionnel Chiappe, Ajaccio ■ 04952 19913 ■ Open Tue–Sat; Sun & Mon D only ■ €€
Charcuterie, *figatellu* (local sausage), roasted goat and sautéed veal with chestnut honey are among the specialities at this restaurant.

See map on p76 ←

🔟 Bonifacio and the South

Bonifacio's chalk cliffs rising abruptly from the sea are an arresting sight, with the medieval town vertiginously crowning the top. Set over a port that looks like a Norwegian fjord, with its wild maquis, the town has an otherworldly atmosphere. Yet for all its charms, Bonifacio is upstaged by nearby Porto-Vecchio, where the shore is strung with magnificent beaches. Inland, a giant wall of hills and pine forest separates the coast from the Alta Rocca, which sprawl into the Golfe de Valinco below the skyline of Sartène.

View across the Îles Lavezzi

BONIFACIO AND THE SOUTH

1 **Top 10 Sights**
see pp85–7

① **Places to Eat**
see p89

① **The Best of the Rest**
see p88

1 Pianu di Levie (Cucuruzzu)

MAP K4 ■ 04957 84821 ■ Open Apr–Oct: 9:30am–6pm (Jun–Sep: to 7pm; Jul & Aug: to 8pm); Nov–Mar: for group bookings only ■ Museum: 04957 80078; Open Jun–Oct: 10am–6pm daily; Oct–May: 10am–5pm Tue–Sat ■ Adm

Savour the atmosphere and distinctive landscape of the Alta Rocca region from the ramparts of this Bronze Age castle, with its vaulted chambers, stairways, hearths and granaries. The site, inhabited around 1400 BC, is set amid an ancient holm oak forest, with views of the distant Aiguilles de Bavella. A 20-minute walk north leads to the A Capula, occupied until 1259, where a Romanesque chapel stands in a clearing. Don't miss Levie's fascinating museum.

2 Sartène

The playwright Prosper Mérimée famously dubbed Sartène (see pp18–19) as "the most Corsican of Corsican towns" – though whether he was referring to its austere appearance or the grim-faced demeanour of its inhabitants is a moot point. Enjoy an apéritif on the ancient place Porta, where locals congregate for a post-prandial walk, then wander around the narrow back alleys. The town's museum boasts the island's largest collection of prehistoric artifacts.

Bonifacio, perched on a clifftop

3 Bonifacio

On a narrow precipice high over the blue waters of the Straits, this old Genoese town (see pp20–21) withstood repeated sieges by the Aragonese and, in 1554, a Turkish fleet led by the corsair Dragut (see p35). The dramatic harbour, clifftop Citadelle and chalk escarpments bring visitors year round. From July to September its cobbled alleyways are often overrun with daytrippers – all the more reason to take an excursion boat out of the port below to view the haute ville from sea level.

4 Îles Lavezzi

MAP L7

This cluster of low granite-rock islets off Bonifacio rests amid superbly transparent water. Boats shuttle here throughout the day in season, allowing plenty of time for snorkelling and for exploring the archipelago's winding pathways and hidden coves. The only structures of note are the walled Cimetière Archiano, where victims of the 1855 shipwreck of the Sémillante (see p21) are buried, and a memorial to the disaster. Bring refreshments along, as there are no cafés on the islands.

The pretty town of Sartène

5 Alta Rocca
MAP K4

The hilly interior of southern Corsica is known as the Alta Rocca. With its deep river valleys, lush chestnut and oak forests and ancient granite villages, it is a world away from the coast. The old paved mule trails and the Mare a Mare Sud hiking route (see p56) are a great way to explore the area, but you can also cover the highlights in a day-long driving tour, stopping for swims, woodland strolls and charcuterie along the way.

Mela, a village in the Alta Rocca

6 Porto-Vecchio
MAP L5

The Genoese developed Porto-Vecchio in 1539 as a harbour from which to ship Corsican cork to the Italian mainland. Afflicted by malaria-carrying mosquitoes, it was eventually abandoned, but has seen a resurgence since World War II, owing to

> **GROUPER FISH**
>
> The clear waters in the Straits of Bonifacio are home to a large colony of extraordinary fish. Tamed by decades of visits, the shoal of grouper used to take morsels from divers' hands, a practice that has been banned. The colony is protected as part of the Réserve Naturelle des Bouches de Bonifacio.

its proximity to some of the island's finest beaches. Chic boutiques pitched at high-rolling Italians line the *haute ville's* medieval streets, which converge at the St Jean-Baptiste and the cheerful Place de la République, filled with cafés and ice-cream shops.

7 Golfe de Valinco

The serene beaches on both the northern and southern shores of the Golfe de Valinco (see pp16–17) are the main reason people base themselves in the southwest of the island, but there are many interesting sights inland to tempt you away from the coast – not least the famous prehistoric site of Filitosa. Catch an excursion boat from Propriano to explore this area's wild coves. Look out for the Genoese watchtowers, a legacy of the pirate raids which forced the local population into the hills in the 15th and 16th centuries.

A view of the harbour of Porto-Vecchio, Corsica

8 Aiguilles de Bavella
MAP K4

Rising from the Corsican watershed on the opposite side of the valley from Monte Incudine, the Aiguilles de Bavella are giant towers of granite. The stacks are visible for miles around, lending a serrated appearance to the skyline inland from Porto-Vecchio. Yellow waymarks flag a scrambling route up to and around the bases – a variant of the GR20 trekking trail, for which the needles provide a stunning closing stretch.

Plage de Palombaggia

9 Plage de Palombaggia
MAP L6

The turquoise water and soft white sand at Palombaggia make for a picture-perfect setting. The beach here actually comprises three contiguous bays, separated by headlands crowned by clumps of umbrella and maritime pines. Palombaggia is the most northerly of the trio and the best for watersports; next comes Tamaricciu, with its stylish café-restaurant made of teak; and finally, Accario, the smallest and quietest.

10 Route de Bavella
MAP L3

One of Corsica's most scenic roads, the route de Bavella winds inland from Solenzara on the southeast coast, approaching the Aiguilles via a series of cliffs, forests and gorges. Despite attempts to widen the road, slow-moving vehicles impede progress in high season, so try to get an early start.

ROUTE DE BAVELLA AND MASSIF DE L'OSPÉDALE

▶ MORNING

This circular driving tour takes in the scenic highlights of the mountain area inland from **Porto-Vecchio**. Leave town on the main Bastia road (T10) and follow it as far as Solenzara, where the D268 turns left off the highway, winding southwest above the Solenzara river. A striking panorama of forested mountains and cliffs is revealed at the Col de Larone. From there onwards, the landscape grows more spectacular at each bend, culminating at the Col de Bavella itself, where, in the shadow of the famous **Aiguilles de Bavella**, you can follow a delightful waymarked trail through pine forest to the **Trou de la Bombe** (see p57), before refuelling with a typical Corsican mountain lunch at the **Auberge du Col de Bavella** (see p89).

AFTERNOON

A white Notre-Dame-des-Neiges (Our Lady of the Snow) statue presides over the high point of the pass, from where the D268 winds downhill all the way to **Zonza** (see p44), one of the prettiest villages in the high Alta Rocca. From Zonza, follow the D368 into the wooded Massif de l'Ospédale. Beyond the Bocca d'Illarata pass, a café on the left side of the road marks the start of a 90-minute walk to the 70-m (230-ft) Piscia di Gallu waterfall. At Ospédale, the next village on the D368, the La Terrace café has superb views across to Sardinia.

See map on p84 ←

The Best of the Rest

Kayakers at Piantarella

① Piantarella
MAP L7

This kayaking, kitesurfing and sailboarding hot spot to the east of Bonifacio encompasses the clearest water on the island.

② Plage de Pinarello
MAP L5

Shallow, pale-blue water, enfolded by a crescent of white sand, makes Pinarello a most attractive beach for families. Easily accessible by road, it gets busy in peak season.

③ Quenza
MAP K4

Over 1,000 years old, this is a quintessential Alta Rocca village, where the broad-leaf forest ebbs into the high uplands of the Coscione plateau. A chapel stands on its outskirts.

④ Plateau de Coscione
MAP K3

To the north of the Alta Rocca, this upland served as a summer pasture for the region's shepherds for centuries. It now lies deserted, save for the odd walker and horse rider.

⑤ Carbini
MAP K5

Carbini, at the foot of the Massif de l'Ospédale, is the site of the Pisan church of San Giovanni where, in 1362, a heretical sect was slaughtered on the orders of the Pope.

⑥ Cala di l'Avena
MAP H6

A broad bay lashed by surf Cala di l'Avena is ideal if you like wild and windy beaches (see p19). A no-frills campsite behind it provides the essentials.

⑦ Plage de Tralicetu
MAP J6

You have to negotiate a very rough, 4-km (3-mile) track to reach Tralicetu, one of southern Corsica's most remote and unspoiled beaches.

⑧ Castellu d'Araggio
MAP L6

High on a rocky hillside to the northwest of Porto-Vecchio, this prehistoric citadel enjoys a spectacular setting, with magnificent views extending across the coast.

⑨ Plage de Balistra
MAP L7

This is the only beach in the Porto-Vecchio–Bonifacio area where you can be assured plenty of room even at the height of summer. Brave the badly rutted piste to get here.

⑩ Ermitage de la Trinité
MAP K7

Huddled beneath a huge granite outcrop, the Ermitage de la Trinité is among the oldest Christian monuments on Corsica. A superb vista extends down the coast.

Ermitage de la Trinité

Places to Eat

① Cantina Doria
MAP K7 ▪ 27 Rue Doria, Bonifacio ▪ 04957 35049 ▪ Open Mar–Oct ▪ €€

Enjoy quality Corsican cuisine, in this restaurant, squeezed into an alley in the *haute ville*.

② Les Quatre Vents
MAP K7 ▪ 29 Quai Banda del Ferro, Bonifacio ▪ 06116 39253, 04957 30750 ▪ Open Wed–Sun ▪ Closed mid-Dec–mid-Feb ▪ €€

Some of Bonifacio's best seafood and bouillabaisse are served in this restaurant overlooking the water. Booking is essential in high season.

Beachside dining at Le Tamaricciu

③ Le Tamaricciu
MAP L6 ▪ Plage Palombaggia, Porto-Vecchio ▪ 04957 04989 ▪ Open mid-Apr–mid-Oct: L; Jun–Aug: D (by reservation only) ▪ €€€

This beach bistro is known for fresh salads, pasta dishes, wood-grilled fish and (at lunchtime) pizzas.

④ Casadelmar
MAP L5 ▪ Rte de Palombaggia, near Porto-Vecchio ▪ 04957 23434 ▪ Open Apr–Oct: D only Tue–Sat; Jul–Aug: Mon–Sat ▪ €€€

Sample the culinary delights crafted by two-Michelin-starred chef Fabio Bragagnolo here (see p66).

⑤ Le Lido
MAP J5 ▪ 42 Av Napoléon III, Propriano ▪ 04957 60637 ▪ Open May–mid-Oct: D ▪ €€€

The spectacular views here are matched by the food, with fresh, creative takes on island classics.

⑥ Bergerie d'Acciola
MAP J5 ▪ Orasi, route de Bonifacio, 8 km south of Sartène ▪ 04957 71400 ▪ Open Jun–Sep: D ▪ €

A terrace restaurant serving great regional dishes with an emphasis on local ewe's and goat's cheese.

⑦ Auberge du Col de Bavella
MAP L4 ▪ Col de Bavella, Zonza ▪ 04957 20987 ▪ Open Apr–Oct ▪ €€

GR20 walkers refuel here on peasant soup, mountain charcuterie, grilled lamb and freshly made desserts.

⑧ Jardin de l'Échaugette
MAP J5 ▪ Place Vardiola, Rue Petrajo, Sartène ▪ 04957 71286, 06204 07149 ▪ Open mid-April–Sep ▪ €€

Enjoy local specialities such as veal stew with chestnut polenta at perhaps this relaxing eatery.

⑨ U Sirenu
MAP J5 ▪ Orasi, Route de Bonifacio, Sartène ▪ 04957 72185, 06243 43846 ▪ €€

The setting is gorgeous, the terrace lovely and the local Corsican grilled meats succulent. There is a pool, too.

⑩ A Pignata
MAP K4 ▪ Route du Pianu, Levie ▪ 04957 84190 ▪ Open Apr–Nov ▪ €€

Enjoy splendid views across the Alta Rocca and rustic cooking at this farmhouse (see p66). Booking is essential.

See map on p84 ←

🔟 Corte, the Interior and the East Coast

If you never venture from the coast, your impression of Corsica will be distorted. Inland, the deep, forested valleys of the island's core create a radical shift in tone. Spilling from the foot of a citadel, Corte is the largest town in Corsica's interior. Its *haute ville*, a warren of red-tiled tenements and churches, presides over a nexus of several major valleys, making it the perfect springboard for treks into the mountains. The quickest route to Corte is via Aléria on the east coast. A broad, flat, low-lying plain striped with vineyards and fruit orchards, this may be the least spectacular side of the island, but it compensates for its scenic shortcomings with some impressive Roman ruins, glorious mountain villages and a vast expanse of relatively unfrequented beaches.

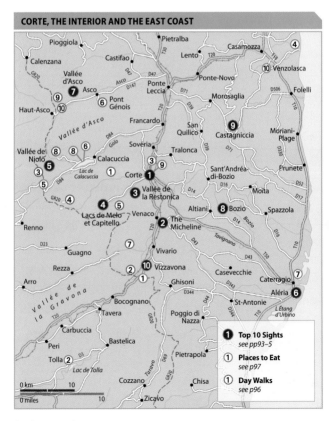

CORTE, THE INTERIOR AND THE EAST COAST

1	**Top 10 Sights**	see pp93–5
1	**Places to Eat**	see p97
1	**Day Walks**	see p96

Previous pages Corte

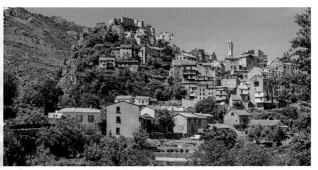

Houses crowd the verdant hillside at Corte

1 Corte

Corte (see pp32–3) served as the island's capital between 1755 and 1769, when Pascal Paoli made it the seat of his revolutionary government. With its imposing mountain backdrop and Moor's Head flags above an 18th-century old town, Corte still retains an aura of nationalist defiance. Bullet holes made by Genoese beseigers pockmark the walls of the cobbled square below the Citadelle, where Corsican-speaking students from the nearby university crowd the bars in term time.

2 The Micheline

Known affectionately as the "Micheline", Corsica's little train is an essential, year-round, all-weather link between Ajaccio and Bastia (see p106). The route, built in the 19th century and upgraded in 2008, is breathtakingly scenic – especially the stretch branching northwest to Calvi from Ponte Leccia, which skirts the fabulous Balagne coastline. Catch one of the four daily services to Vizzavona from Corte – a 40-minute ride through pine forests and pretty villages, including a crossing of the famous Pont de Vecchiu bridge.

3 Vallée de la Restonica
MAP D6

Mesmerized by the high ridges above them, few visitors to the Vallée de la Restonica (see p32) spare more than a passing glance at the valley floor, but the river surging across it hides dozens of superb swimming spots. The pale-green meltwater cascades through pools hollowed from immense granite boulders called "vasques". Shady areas under the Laricio pines make perfect picnic spots, while a network of old shepherds' trails provides a great opportunity for a walk around the forest.

Stream in Vallée de la Restonica

4 Lacs de Melo et Capitello
MAP D7

The Vallée de la Restonica scythes from the outskirts of Corte into the heart of the watershed – one of the Mediterranean's great mountain wildernesses. In summer, visitors drive or catch the shuttle bus to the car park at the end of the valley, from where a trail leads to two beautiful glacial lakes, surrounded by a vast stadium of cliffs. Visit before the snow melts in early May to see the lakes partly frozen.

5 Vallée de Niolo
MAP C6

Corsica's most remote mountain region is the Vallée de Niolo. Its focal point, below the eroded southern fringes of Monte Cinto *(see p55)*, is a broad depression scattered with granite villages where vestiges of the old transhumant culture that once held sway here are still discernible. The local ewe's cheese is mouth-wateringly good, and the walking is superlative. If you are in the area in September, do not miss the annual fair, A Santa di u Niolu *(see p71)*.

Calacuccia in the Vallée de Niolo

6 Aléria
MAP M1

At the mouth of the Tavignano river on the eastern coastal plain, Aléria was a major Greek and Roman colony in ancient times, when the Étang de Diane lagoon below was the island's main harbour and naval base. Ruins of the former Roman town (closed Sun in Nov–Mar), which include baths, a forum, triumphal archway and archaeological museum, are spread over a hilltop to the south of the modern village. Foodies can dine on oysters from the nearby *étang* (pond).

CORSICAN POLYPHONY

Corsica boasts its own distinctive brand of choral music – known locally as "polyphonies corses". The style, which hinges on three or four parts, evolved a means of singing Mass in remote shepherds' villages, but has since become the backbone of a vibrant and popular musical revival led by groups such as I Muvrini and A Filetta *(see p73)*.

7 Vallée d'Asco
MAP C5

The head of the Asco Valley, known as Haut-Asco, is flanked by Corsica's highest mountains, including Monte Cinto. It was here, amid the pines and boulder moraines, that Felix von Cube and the other early pioneers of Corsican mountaineering made their base camp in the 1900s, while forging routes up the peaks. The wood-lined bar in the ski station here displays antique photos of the explorers and you can admire the awesome crags opposite from Le Chalet's terrace.

8 Bozio
MAP E7

This micro-region, overlooking the Vallée du Tavignano *(see p32)* to the southeast of Corte, sees very few visitors but is a great area for getting a feel of traditional mountain life. Along what was the old via Romana, a string of picturesque stone villages looks across the valley to Monte Rotondo. The Mare a Mare Centre hiking trail winds through deserted uplands and ruined sheepfolds.

9 Castagniccia
MAP E5

Swathed in a dense canopy of chestnut forest, Castagniccia, in the northeast of the island, has an entirely different feel to it. The intense greenery ensures a moist climate and in autumn, when the woods are ablaze with colour, mist cloaks the valley floor most mornings. Splendid Baroque

Mountain village in Castagniccia

churches, great walks around the forest and the pungent local charcuterie draw visitors here.

⑩ Vizzavona
MAP K1

A collection of tin-roofed railway buildings and forestry huts, Vizzavona is the highest stop on Corsica's diminutive train line – a perfect springboard for walks in the magnificent Laricio pine forest. Picnickers meander through the woods to the Cascade des Anglais waterfall (see p60), while those with more stamina and a head for heights scale the Monte d'Oro, whose grey-blue cliffs and pointed summit are this area's defining landmark.

Hikers in Vizzavona

A DRIVE THROUGH CORSICA'S INTERIOR

▶ MORNING

This circular route loops through some of the least visited, but most scenic corners of central and eastern Corsica. Begin by heading south from **Corte** (see p93) on the main Ajaccio highway (T20). After 33 km (21 miles), just beyond Vivario, turn left on to the D69 at the **Col de la Serra Piana** (see p96) to start the ascent of the 1311-m- (4,300-ft-) high Col de Sorba. An 11-km (7-mile) drop down the other side brings you to the dramatically sited village of Ghisoni, where there's a great café to make an atmospheric pit stop. From Ghisoni, follow the D344 as it winds through the awesome Défilé de Strette gorge to Ste-Antoine, where you should turn left and follow the D343 across the vineyards to **Aléria**. Tour the hilltop Roman ruins and adjacent museum before heading east to the nearby Plage du Padulone for a swim and bite to eat at one of the beachside *paillotes* (huts). Then continue northwest from Aléria on the T50, turning right on to the D14 after 13 km (8 miles).

AFTERNOON

This tortuous road follows the course of the old via Romana through the wonderful **Bozio** region – among the most spectacular drives on the island. Head through Pietraserena, Altiani and Erbajolo villages, before dropping back down to the valley floor via the D14. This brings you out on the T50, only 5 km (3 miles) south of Corte.

See map on p92 ←

Day Walks

Gorges du Tavignano

1 Gorges du Tavignano
MAP C7

Follow the zigzagging Genoese mule track up this valley near Corte to reach an awesome gorge, carpeted with Laricio pines. Chanterelle mushrooms grow in profusion here in autumn.

2 Cascade des Anglais
MAP K1

Accessed via a gentle 20-minute amble through a pine forest, this idyllic waterfall is a perfect spot for a picnic, with plenty of pools to splash about in nearby.

3 Cascades de Radule
MAP C6

The landscape starts to feel like a mountain as you approach the hidden Radule waterfall, just off the GR20 in the Golo river valley. The start point is the car park at Col de Vergio.

4 Lac de Nino
MAP C7

Scramble up the steep sides of the Vallée de Niolo to reach the largest and most beautiful of Corsica's many glacial lakes, suspended in the middle of green pasture, against a magnificent mountain backdrop.

5 Lac d'Oriente
MAP D7

The challenging climb up Monte Rotondo may be only for confirmed mountaineering enthusiasts, but this magical glacial lake halfway up is more easily accessible.

6 Col de la Serra Piana
MAP D5

Swim under the old Pont d'Asco Genoese bridge before climbing the side valley opposite Asco village to reach a lonely pass with great views.

7 Gorges de Manganellu
MAP D7

Follow the orange waymarks from the hamlet of Canaglia, 25 km (16 miles) south of Corte, to reach one of the island's loveliest forested valleys. The remote Bergerie de Tolla is the perfect turnaround point.

8 Pont de Muricciolu
MAP C6

On the outskirts of Albertacce village, a Genoese packhorse bridge spans a particularly photogenic stretch of river. Huge, water-worn slabs flank the river, which you can reach in an easy half hour's walk.

9 Punta Muvrella
MAP C5

The "Peak of the Sheep" is a superb eagle's nest summit overlooking the Vallée d'Asco (see p94) to the Cinto Massif. It is a relentlessly steep three-hour, 700-m (2,296-ft) climb from the Haut-Asco ski station.

10 Tour des Cinque Frati
MAP C6

This is a classic walk in the Vallée de Niolo (see p94), looping around a phalanx of rock pinnacles. Leaflets detailing the route are on sale at local tourist offices.

Places to Eat

1 Monte d'Oro
MAP K1 ▪ Vivario, near Vizzavona ▪ 04954 72106, 06143 63607 ▪ Open May–Sep ▪ €€

Try traditional mountain cooking at this famous wayside restaurant *(see p66)*, where the main Ajaccio–Bastia highway crosses the watershed.

2 Bergerie de Tolla
MAP K1 ▪ Gorges de Manganellu ▪ Open mid-Jun–mid-Sep ▪ €

This sheepfold in the forest serves delicious ewe's cheese omelettes.

3 Auberge de la Restonica
MAP D6 ▪ Route de Restonica, 2 km southwest of Corte ▪ 04954 60958 ▪ Open Apr–Oct ▪ €€

Quality Corsican mountain cuisine, such as fresh trout stuffed with mint, is served at this romantic hotel.

Rustic interior of U Fragnu

4 U Fragnu
MAP F5 ▪ U Campu, Route de Vescovato, Venzolasca ▪ 04953 66233 ▪ €€

This bistro, specializing in Corsican cuisine, serves huge portions of veal and olive stew, soup with fresh soft cheese and leek and *brocciu* fritters.

5 "U Cintu" Chez Jojo
MAP C6 ▪ Albertacce, Vallée de Niolo ▪ 04954 80687 ▪ €

Sample charcuterie, rich game stews and chestnut flour desserts in this simple village eatery next to the Calacuccia lake. Food is great value.

PRICE CATEGORIES

For a three-course meal for one with half a bottle of wine (or equivalent meal), taxes and extra charges.

€ under €30   €€ €30–50   €€€ over €50

6 Restaurant du Lac
MAP C6 ▪ Sidossi, near Calacuccia, Vallée de Niolo ▪ 04954 80273 ▪ €

Sample down-to-earth Nioline dishes flavoured with wild mountain herbs, mushrooms and cheese.

7 Aux Coquillages de Diana
MAP M1 ▪ Étang de Diana, Aléria ▪ 04955 70455 ▪ Open May–Sep: daily; Oct–Apr: lunch daily, dinner Fri & Sat ▪ Closed Jan ▪ €€

Shellfish aficionados can tuck into local Nustale oysters and mussels, washed down with Vermentino wine.

8 Restaurant de l'Ampugnani
MAP E5 ▪ La Porta, Castagniccia ▪ 04953 92200 ▪ Open 11:30am–10pm daily ▪ €

Savour Castagniccian trout, free-range pork stews and crunchy *brocciu beignets* in this dining salon that also offers lovely valley views.

9 Osteria di l'Orta
MAP D6 ▪ Casa Guelfucci, Pont de l'Orta, Corte ▪ 04956 10641 ▪ Open Apr–Sep: Mon–Fri ▪ €€

Corsican specialities, such as veal with olives and a chestnut mousse, entice diners to this restaurant in an 18th-century mansion.

10 L'Ortu
MAP F5 ▪ Route de Venzolasca, Vescovato ▪ 04953 66469 ▪ Open May–Sep: Wed–Sun ▪ €

This organic farm-restaurant specializes in vegetarian fare made with their own and locally sourced produce. The odd free-range pork dish is offered for die-hard carnivores.

See map on p92

TOP 10 Bastia and the North

With its rugged interior and turquoise water-fringed coastline, the far north of Corsica, stretching from Bastia to Calvi via Cap Corse, confirms most of the clichés usually ascribed to the island. There

is barely a patch of flat ground in the entire region. Journeys tend to be winding and take longer than you would expect, but reveal astonishing landscapes at every bend. The Italian influence is slightly more marked in the north too, especially around Bastia, where the Genoese-built Vieux Port could have been transported in its entirety from the Ligurian coast, visible on clear days across the Tyrrhenian Sea. The Genoese were also responsible for the most striking man-made landmark of the far north: Calvi's Citadelle, whose ochre walls preside over a magnificent panorama of sea and granite mountains.

The impressive ceiling of Bastia Cathedral

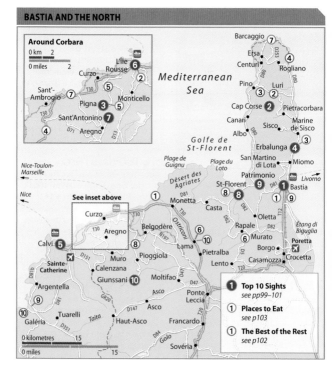

BASTIA AND THE NORTH

Around Corbara

0 km 2
0 miles 2

Curzo · L'Île Rousse 6
Sant'-Ambrogio 7 · T30 · Monticello 5
Pigna 3 5
Sant'Antonino 7
4 · D71 · Aregno · D13

Mediterranean Sea

Barcaggio 7
Ersa
Centuri · 4 · Rogliano
Pino
Luri 2
Cap Corse 2 · Pietracorbara
Canari
Albo · Sisco · Marine de Sisco 3
Golfe de St-Florent
San Martino di Lota · Miomo
Plage de Guignu · Plage du Loto
Patrimonio · Livorno
Désert des Agriates
St-Florent 9 8 · Bastia 1 9
Monetta
Casta
Oletta
Curzo
Belgodère 6 · Rapale · Murato 6 · Étang di Biguglia
Aregno
Lama · Pietralba · Borgo
Calvi 5
Muro · Pioggiola · Lento · Casamozza · Crocetta
Sainte Catherine · Calenzana
Argentella · Giunssani 10 · Moltifao
9 · Asco · Ponte Leccia
Galéria 10 · Tuarelli · Asco
Haut-Asco · Francardo
Sovéria

Nice-Toulon-Marseille
Nice
See inset above

1 **Top 10 Sights**
see pp99–101

1 **Places to Eat**
see p103

1 **The Best of the Rest**
see p102

0 kilometres 15
0 miles 15

Bastia's picturesque Vieux Port

1 Bastia

Bastia (see pp22–3) is the island's main centre of commerce and culture. Despite the fact that Napoleon made his home town Ajaccio the official capital, Bastia has a more citified atmosphere than its rival. For visitors, the Vieux Port district of Terra Vecchia, and the Citadelle district of Terra Nova overlooking it, form the principal focus. The Second Empire thoroughfares across town have many places to shop.

2 Cap Corse

Plunging sheer into the sea, the western flank of the Cap Corse peninsula (see pp26–7) is steep and relatively inhospitable, with schist-roofed hamlets clinging to the few balconies of level land above tiny harbours. The eastern side, however, has a gentler feel. Terraced vineyards, founded five centuries ago by the Genoese, cascade to a slither of undulating shoreline. It takes a day to round the cape by car, an experience not to be missed.

3 Pigna
MAP C4

The sky-blue woodwork and immaculately pointed masonry testify to Pigna's government-funded renaissance as a centre for local arts and crafts. A dozen or more studios operate here, selling ceramics, musical boxes, bamboo flutes and Corsican citterns, among other things. Pigna's main hotel-restaurant, Casa Musicale (see p103) is a major centre for traditional Balagne music.

4 Erbalunga
MAP F3

Only 9 km (6 miles) north of Bastia, the fishing port of Erbalunga (see p27) has almost become a suburb of the city – albeit one with a distinct identity of its own. The picturesque harbour's entrance is guarded by a stalwart watchtower, and Le Pirate restaurant (see p103) nearby serves excellent seafood. Erbalunga is also known across the island for its sombre Good Friday procession of masked penitents, La Cerca (see p70), a sight well worth catching if you are in the area.

Erbalunga harbour and watchtower

An aerial view over Calvi and out to sea

5 Calvi

Calvi's spectacular setting *(see pp30–31)* has lured visitors since the early days of tourism in the region. Its attractions include a glamorous marina, a few Baroque churches and the house claimed locally to be the birthplace of Christopher Columbus. The highlight is the glorious vision of the Genoese Citadelle, framed by its backdrop of brilliant-blue sea and distant mountains.

Lighthouse and tower at L'Île Rousse

6 L'Île Rousse
MAP C4

Founded by Pascal Paoli in 1765, L'Île Rousse has thrived ever since, particularly after its rebirth as a French Riviera-style resort. Midway along the Balagne coast, the red isle from which the town derives its name rises to the north, and a superb view extends from its lighthouse across the rooftops to the hills beyond.

7 Sant'Antonino
MAP C4

The constellation of pastel-washed, orange- and pink-granite villages strewn over the hillsides immediately inland from L'Île Rousse and Calvi – an area known as the Balagne – are ranked among the prettiest in the Mediterranean; and Sant'Antonino *(see p45)* is widely regarded as the most picturesque of them all. Its warren of narrow, cobbled alleyways crowd like a bird's nest on the conical summit of a hill, affording visitors a dramatic panoramic view of the surrounding sea and hills.

CAP CORSE MUSCAT

The famous muscat wine **(below)** produced in the vineyards of Cap Corse, made from a sweet, aromatic grape, has been a speciality of the region since Genoese times. The fruit is partially sun-dried to intensify the sugars before being pressed. Fermentation occurs later with an infusion of pure alcohol.

8 St-Florent

The absence of a white-sand beach within easy driving distance of the town has left the cluster of slate-tiled fishermen's houses packed around St-Florent's Citadelle delightfully unspoiled. There are some magnificent beaches across the gulf, such as the plage du Loto, but you have to jump on a boat to get to them. The waterfront, lined with cafés, is truly atmospheric at sunset, when the Tenda hills behind turn molten red *(see pp28–9)*.

Patrimonio, surrounded by vineyards

9 Patrimonio

The Genoese exported vast quantities of wine from Patrimonio – mostly sweet, blossom-scented muscat. A few thousand hectares of vines remain under cultivation on the leeward side of the village's striking chalk escarpments, although today Patrimonio *(see p27)* is synonymous with its superb dry reds. In the shadow of the village church, numerous wine *caves* offer tastings.

10 Giunssani
MAP C5

Given its proximity to the Balagne coast, it is amazing how few visitors venture into the beautiful Giunssani region, just over the mountain from L'Île Rousse. A hidden Shangri-La of pristine chestnut and pine forest, crashing streams and wonderful scenery, the region is dominated by the awesome profile of the 2,393-m (7,850-ft) high Monte Padro to the south.

A DRIVE AROUND THE CAP CORSE CORNICHE

▶ MORNING

A circuit of the Corniche can be completed in a full day. If you are troubled by local driving styles and the sheer drops, follow it in a clockwise direction, ensuring you stay on the landward side of the road. Begin by heading out of **Bastia** *(see pp22–3)* on the D81, which crosses the ridge at windswept Col de Teghime, where a marvellous view over the Nebbio and bay is revealed. Stop for a coffee and croissant in the **Place des Portes** *(see p28)* in **St-Florent** *(see pp28–9)*, then proceed northwards through the vineyards of **Patrimonio** towards **Nonza** *(see p26)*, where the Genoese watchtower affords another stupendous view – this time west over the bay to the Désert des Agriate coast. The shoreline grows noticeably wilder as you press north. Pause at pretty **Centuri Port** *(see p27)* for a stroll around its little lobster-fishing harbour, then begin the zigzagging ascent of the Cap's northern tip to reach Barcaggio via the D253. Stop for lunch at the **U Fanale** restaurant *(see p103)*.

AFTERNOON

From Barcaggio, continue west to **Macinaggio** *(see p26)*, from where excursion boats run up the wild coastline further north. The remaining leg down the east coast of the Cap is an easier drive; be sure to stock up on fine muscat at the **Domaine Pieretti** vineyard en route *(see p69)*.

See map on p98 ←

The Best of the Rest

The golden sands of plage de l'Ostriconi

 Plage de l'Ostriconi
MAP C3

This sweep of honey-coloured sand and jade-green water is at the northwestern edge of the Désert des Agriate.

2 A Mimoria di u Vinu
MAP E2 ▪ Place San Petru, Luri ▪ 04953 10232 ▪ Call for opening hours ▪ Adm

This small, community-run museum near Luri showcases the region's wine industry.

 Tour de Sénèque
Crowning the Cap Corse watershed, this remote tower makes a fine vantage point *(see p26)*.

 Boat Trip
MAP F1 ▪ San Paulu, Port de Plaisance, Macinaggio ▪ 04953 50709 ▪ Boats depart May–Sep: 11am, 2pm (Jul & Aug: also 4:15pm) ▪ Adm ▪ www.sanpaulu.com

This 2-hour trip cruises past the Îles Finnachiarola bird colony, making swimming stops en route.

 Corbara
MAP C4

Corbara is famed for one of the island's most lavish Baroque churches, the Annonciation (open 3–6pm). The artifacts at the village's Musée Privé are also worth a look.

 Lama
MAP D4 ▪ 04954 82404 ▪ Adm

As its grand period houses underline, Lama formerly ranked among the Balagne's most prosperous villages. It is now a sleepy backwater albeit a very pretty one.

 Algajola
MAP C4

Packed around the western end of a broad, sandy beach, the village of Algajola numbers among Corsica's pleasant low-key seaside resorts.

 Speloncato
MAP C4

Extending to the distant sea, the view over the pale terracotta rooftops of Speloncato is one of the most famous in the Balagne region.

9 Vallée du Fango
MAP B6

The grandest of the valleys cutting into Corsica's interior from the Balagne coast, Fango ends abruptly at Paglia Orba's north face.

10 Galéria
MAP B5

The final outpost of the Balagne before the coast road begins its long climb to the Col de la Palmarella and Golfe de Porto, this remote fishing village is near several quiet beaches.

Places to Eat

1 **La Table du Marché**
MAP P5 ▪ Pl du Marché, Bastia
▪ 04953 16425 ▪ Closed Sun ▪ €€€
This terrace restaurant on Bastia's 18th-century market square is the place to try fresh local delicacies.

2 **Le Pasquale Paoli**
MAP C4 ▪ 2 Place Paoli, L'Île Rousse ▪ 04954 76770 ▪ Open May–mid-Oct: Tue–Sat ▪ €€€
This is one of the few restaurants *(see p66)* in Corsica to have a Michelin star for its traditional local cuisine.

3 **Le Pirate**
MAP F3 ▪ Erbalunga, Brando, 12 km north of Bastia ▪ 04953 32420 ▪ Open Apr–mid-Oct ▪ €€€
The last word in gourmet Corsican seafood, Le Pirate *(see p66)* also has a wine list that is second to none.

4 **Le Grand Oggi**
MAP B4 ▪ Hôtel Chez Charles, 32 Route de Bastia, Lumio ▪ 04956 06171 ▪ Open Apr–Nov: D only ▪ €€€
High above the Golfe de Calvi in Lumio, this glitzy hotel-restaurant *(see p66)* has a menu as enticing as the views.

5 **Casa Musicale**
MAP C4 ▪ Place de l'Église, Pigna ▪ 04956 17731 ▪ Closed Jan–mid-Feb ▪ €€
Delicious food, made using organic and locally sourced ingredients, is served here.

Terrace at Casa Musicale

PRICE CATEGORIES
For a three-course meal for one with half a bottle of wine (or equivalent meal), taxes and extra charges.

€ under €30   €€ €30–€50   €€€ over €50

6 **Ferme-Auberge Campo di Monte**
MAP E4 ▪ Murato ▪ 04953 76439 ▪ Open Jun–mid-Sep: D only; mid-Sep–May: L Thu–Sun ▪ €€
Enjoy veal ragout and courgette fritters at this farmhouse *(see p66)* hidden on a remote Nebbio mountain-side. Reservations are essential.

7 **U Fanale**
MAP E1 ▪ Barcaggio, Cap Corse ▪ 04953 56272 ▪ Open Apr–Oct ▪ €€
A more inspiring menu than most at the northern end of the Cap, and the perfect location on the water's edge. Try the grouper curry with apple sauce.

8 **La Roya**
MAP E3 ▪ Hotel de la Roya, Rte de la Plage, St-Florent ▪ 04953 70040 ▪ Open late Mar–mid-Nov ▪ €€€
St-Florent's most elegant restaurant *(see p66)* is in a modern three-star hotel. Chef Michel Lenco is famous for seafood, but the seasonal menu also features orsican meat dishes.

9 **U Paisanu**
MAP P7 ▪ 9 Rue Monseigneur Rigo, Bastia ▪ 04953 62092, 06313 00193 ▪ Open Wed– Sat ▪ D only ▪ €€
An intimate restaurant with its own charcuterie boutique, U Paisanu serves traditional Corsican cuisine. Reservations recommended.

10 **Campu Latinu**
MAP D4 ▪ Lama ▪ 06092 04753, 04954 82383 ▪ Open May–Sep: D only ▪ €€
Dine alfresco under the oaks on the stone terraces of this restaurant, which overlooks the village of Lama. Their "menu corse" is great value.

See map on p98

Streetsmart

Exterior of a bakery in L'Île Rousse

Getting To and Around Corsica

Arriving by Air

Corsica has four airports handling international and domestic flights. **Napoleon Bonaparte Airport** (Ajaccio) and **Bastia-Poretta** are the busiest, followed by **Calvi Ste-Catherine** and **Figari-Corse Sud**.

Air France and its subsidiary carrier **Air Corsica** operate scheduled flights to Corsica from mainland France, with direct services from Paris, Marseille, Nice, Bordeaux, Toulouse and Lyon. Scheduled flights from the UK involve at least one change, usually in Paris or at a Riviera airport, and are more expensive than travelling with a low-cost carrier or charter. **EasyJet** fly to Ajaccio and Bastia from various airports in the UK and other European cities, and **Flybe** flies to Bastia.

If you are not hiring a car, there is a shuttle bus (TCA Bus No. 8) that connects Ajaccio airport to the train station. Similarly, the city bus service in Bastia (**STIB**) links Bastia airport to its train station. There are no shuttles from Figari or Calvi airports. Some hotels offer transfers; otherwise it's a good idea to arrange in advance for a pick-up with **Suntransfers** or a taxi, especially if your flight arrives in the evening.

Arriving by Sea

Ferries sail from many ports on the French and Italian Rivieras and from neighbouring islands.

Services to Ajaccio and Bastia from Nice, Toulon and Marseille are most frequent, but you can also take boats to L'Île Rousse in the north and Propriano and Porto-Vecchio in the south. Popular ferry companies include **Corsica Ferries**, **Mobylines** and **La Meridionale**.

Travelling by Train

Small local trains connect the towns of Ajaccio, Bastia, Corte, Calvi and L'Île Rousse. For up-to-date information on schedules and fares, check the websites of **CF** (Chemins de Fer de la Corse) or **Train Corse**.

Travelling by Bus

Corsica's bus network, privately run by several different firms, is not very well integrated. While services between major towns are frequent, those to outlying regions are often designed to coincide with school timetables so buses may not depart at convenient times. Check the **Corsica Bus** website for schedules.

Travelling by Car

Driving is the best way to get around, although the mountainous terrain, narrow roads and profusion of impatient Corsican motorists can be intimidating. As a courtesy, pull over when possible to allow local drivers to overtake.

Car-hire firms **Avis**, **Hertz**, **Europcar** and **Enterprise** have several outlets across the island, including at the airports. Rates range from €280 to €350 per week. Car seats for kids cost extra. Note that queues at the airport can be long when a flight arrives, so head straight to a rental desk once you've reclaimed your baggage.

Filling stations are common along main roads but are scarce on the ground when you are off the beaten track. Check your fuel gauge regularly, and remember that most petrol stations, apart from those near the airports, close on Sundays. In towns, many supermarkets have self-serve 24-hour pumps, provided that your credit card has a chip and PIN.

Rush hours only affect Corsica's larger towns, where they can be frustrating. With workers returning home for their midday meal, rush hour can occur four times a day. Getting to and from popular beaches may prove a stop-and-start affair in peak season.

Pay car parks have become the norm in some villages and at beaches, where you will usually have to pay between €3 and €8 to leave your vehicle.

Travelling by Taxi

There are taxi firms in every major town. All taxis have meters, but for longer trips, it's best to come to an understanding on the fares before setting out.

Travelling by Bicycle

Due to Corsica's steep geography and narrow roads, only keen cyclists accustomed to riding in such conditions should consider getting around the island by bike. It is also wise to avoid the summer months, because of the heat and traffic.

Several firms offer cycling holidays (see p110), taking in scenic routes and arranging accommodation and support.

Travelling on Foot

Long-distance footpaths, superbly waymarked and supported by a network of hostels, traverse the island from coast to coast via its scenic highlights. Many trails go through the **Parc Naturel Régional de Corse** (PNRC). Created in 1972, the park protects nearly 40 per cent of the island's interior wilderness and also maintains Corsica's 1,500-km (932-mile) footpath network.

Every year, walkers are lost in the Corsican mountains after venturing into the wilderness without adequate equipment or navigation skills. Always keep to the waymarked path (sentier balisé), and make sure you have food, water and warm, waterproof clothing in case of a change in weather.

Maps

Google coverage of Corsica is crisp down to 50 m (165 ft), and Streetview coverage is comprehensive. The best printed map is the yellow Michelin 1:200,000. Walkers may also want to buy the IGN 1:25,000 maps for their chosen routes.

Off-Season Travel

All public transport to and from Corsica is reduced between mid-October and Easter. Only skeleton ferry services sail, and many bus routes are suspended.

DIRECTORY

ARRIVING BY AIR

Air Corsica
W aircorsica.com

Air France
W airfrance.com

Bastia-Poretta
22 km (14 miles) southeast of Bastia in Lucciana
C 04955 45454
W bastia.aeroport.fr

Calvi Ste-Catherine
6 km (4 miles) southeast of Calvi
C 04956 58888
W calvi.aeroport.fr

easyJet
W easyjet.com

Figari-Corse Sud
21 km (13 miles) north of Bonifacio C 04957 11010 W 2a.cci.fr

Flybe
W flybe.com

Napoleon Bonaparte Airport
Campo dell'Oro, 7 km (4 miles) east of Ajaccio
C 04952 35656
W 2a.cci.fr

STIB buses (Bastia)
C 04953 10665

Suntransfers
W suntransfers.com

TCA (Ajaccio)
C 04952 32941

ARRIVING BY SEA

Corsica Ferries
W corsica-ferries.co.uk

La Meridionale
W lameridionale.fr

Mobylines
W mobylines.com

TRAVELLING BY TRAIN

CF
W cf-corse.fr

Trains Corse
W train-corse.com

TRAVELLING BY BUS

Corsica Bus
W corsicabus.org

TRAVELLING BY CAR

Avis
W avis.fr

Enterprise
W enterprise.fr

Europcar
W europcar.fr

Hertz
W hertzcorse.com

TRAVELLING BY TAXI

Ajaccio
C 04952 27970
C 06089 66785
W allo-taxis-ajaccio.com

Bastia
C 04953 60465
W corsica-taxis.com

Calvi
C 04956 53036
W radio-taxis-calvais.com

Figari
C 06177 73796
W taxi-sud-corse.com

TRAVELLING ON FOOT

Parc Naturel Régional de Corse
MAP N2 ■ Maison d'Information du PNRC: 2 Rue Major Lambroschini, Ajaccio
W parc-corse.org

Practical Information

Passports and Visas

No visa is required for EU nationals to visit France. Citizens of the US, Canada, Australia, New Zealand and Israel are permitted to visit for a maximum of 3 months without a visa. Everyone is required to carry some form of identification on them at all times. Check the **French Foreign Ministry** website for details.

Customs and Immigration

There is no limit on goods that can be taken into or out of France for visitors from most EU countries. Travellers from outside the EU face heavier restrictions but, unlike EU citizens, are entitled to a limited amount of duty-free purchases.

Travel Safety Advice

Visitors can get up-to-date travel safety information from the **UK Foreign and Commonwealth Office**, the **US Department of State** and the **Australian Department of Foreign Affairs and Trade**.

Travel Insurance

It is a good idea to obtain comprehensive travel insurance that covers both health and personal belongings before going to Corsica. Extra insurance may be required if you are planning to hike the GR20 or participate in extreme sports. EU citizens carrying a valid **EHIC** (European Health Insurance Card) may be reimbursed of a lot of the cost of state-provided medical treatment.

Health

Corsica has good hospitals with accident and emergency facilities.

Pharmacies are identifiable by their prominent green crosses (illuminated at night), and stock a wide range of medicines. EU citizens can redeem the cost of prescriptions from their home health authority.

If you need a dentist, contact your holiday company representative or ask your hotel owner where to go. Costs are comparable with those charged by private practitioners in the UK.

Personal Security

In terms of personal security, take the same precautions you would at home. Always lock your car and keep your valuables in a safe place. Special care, however, should be taken when leaving possessions on crowded beaches.

Any lost property in Corsica is usually handed over to the nearest police station (*gendarmerie*). "Je voudrais recupérer un objet égaré" ("I would like to claim a lost item") is the phrase you'll need. Take along your passport.

The main dangers for swimmers are sea anemones. Their tiny brown spines snap off and get lodged under the skin if trodden on and can rapidly cause inflammation. The same applies to jellyfish: their sting can be painful for an hour or two.

If you do much forest walking, you may come across a wild boar, but you are without risk unless you meet a mother with piglets – in which case, back off as quietly and as quickly as possible.

Mountain enthusiasts should be familiar with the **PGHM** (Peloton des Gendarmes de Haute Montagne) and **GMSP** (Groupe Montagne des Sapeurs-Pompiers), two Corsican Mountain Rescue groups. These groups are comprised of trained experts and are available summer and winter.

Emergency Services

In case of emergencies, if you don't speak French, ring the free **European Emergency** number from your mobile to reach the **police**, **fire** or **ambulance** services. *Au secours* is the French phrase for "help".

Travellers with Specific Needs

While things are improving, Corsica still has some way to go when it comes to accessibility for wheelchair users. French law requires that new and renovated hotels supply at least one room for disabled visitors; if you have special needs, be sure to mention them at the time of booking.

Ferries have adapted cabins, and beaches called *handiplages* are equipped for wheelchair users. For more detailed information, visit the websites of the **APF** Association des Paralysés de France) and **Corsica Access** (in English).

Currency and Banking

Corsica's currency is the euro (€). Bank notes are issued in denominations of 5, 10, 20, 50, 100, 200 and 500. The euro has eight coin denominations of €2, €1, 50 cents, 20 cents, 10 cents, 5 cents, 2 cents and 1 cent.

Standard opening hours or banks are 8am–noon and 2–5pm Mon–Fri. They no longer exchange foreign currency or cash travellers' cheques. All branches offer automatic teller machine (ATM) facilities.

Bank cards are the most convenient and cost-effective way to access your money and to pay for major goods and services. Use your normal debit or credit card to withdraw cash, for which you will be charged a small commission by your bank.

To ensure your first transaction in Corsica isn't declined (a security measure triggered by using the card in a different country), inform your bank of your travel plans. Also take along a spare in case the main card is declined at an ATM.

Telephone and Internet

Many shops, cafés and hotels now offer free Wi-Fi or guests.

Corsica's ten-digit telephone numbers should be dialled in full when phoning from within the island or mainland France. From abroad, dial 00 (the international dialling code) followed by 33 (the code for France) then the ten-digit number minus the first zero.

Your mobile network will automatically connect when you arrive. Coverage is sufficient in all but a handful of black spots in the interior. You may struggle to get a signal in the mountains.

Public telephones are few and far between and require the use of prepaid cards *(cartes téléphoniques)*, available at newsagents.

Postal Services

Distinguished by their yellow-and-blue livery, post offices – *postes* or PTTs – are found in cities, towns and larger villages. In cities, they are open 8am–7pm Mon–Fri and 8am–noon Sat; in smaller towns, 9am–noon and 2–4:45pm Mon–Sat. Stamps are sold at newsagents and tobacconists.

Opening Hours

Opening hours of shops and banks are typically 8:30/9am–1/1:30pm and 2:30/3–6/7pm. These vary according to the business in question. Opening hours for museums, tourist offices and other visitor attractions change according to the season.

Time Difference

Corsica follows Central European Time, one hour ahead of Greenwich Mean Time (GMT). Daylight Saving Time (DST) starts at 3am on the last Sunday in March and finishes at 2am on the last Sunday of October.

DIRECTORY

PASSPORTS AND VISAS

French Foreign Ministry
🌐 diplomatie.gouv.fr

TRAVEL SAFETY ADVICE

Australian Department of Foreign Affairs and Trade
Department of Foreign Affairs and Trade
🌐 dfat.gov.au
🌐 smarttraveller.gov.au

UK Foreign and Commonwealth Office
Foreign and Commonwealth Office
🌐 gov.uk/foreign-travel-advice

US Department of State
US Department of State
🌐 travel.state.gov

TRAVEL INSURANCE

EHIC
🌐 ehic.org.uk

PERSONAL SECURITY

PGHM
📞 04956 11395
📞 112

GMSP
📞 04953 09800

EMERGENCY SERVICES

Ambulance
📞 15

European Emergency (English-speaking)
📞 112

Fire (*Pompiers*)
📞 16

Police (Gendarmes)
📞 17

TRAVELLERS WITH SPECIFIC NEEDS

APF
🌐 apf-corse.blogs.apf.asso.fr

Corsica Access
🌐 corsica-access.org

Electrical Appliances

Electrical current in Corsica is 220v/50Hz AC. Travellers from the UK and North America will need standard round-pin adapters, which are sold at most airports.

Weather

Corsica enjoys classic Mediterranean weather: warm, dry and sunny from June to September, with temperatures reaching an average of 30°C (86°F). In May and September, temperatures hover around 20–25°C (68–77°F). Rainfall is at its highest in October and November, although sudden storms can blow in at any time.

July and August are peak season in Corsica. Temperatures reach their hottest, the beaches and resorts can get very crowded, and prices soar. A far more relaxing time to visit, both in terms of climate and visitor numbers, is May to early June, or mid-September to mid-October.

Visitor Information

The island's official tourist website **Visit Corsica** is packed with information in English. Another useful source of information is the **Corsica Isula** site.

Trips and Tours

Numerous companies, such as **Corsica Aventure** and **Keadventure**, offer specialist walking holidays, including treks along the GR20. While some may only provide basic bed, board and route cards, others offer qualified local mountain guides and full baggage transfer between stages.

Local rock-climbing guides have to pass stringent examinations to become fully accredited and insurable, which means their rates are rather high if you employ them on a daily basis. **Xtreme Sud**, based near the massif de Bavella, is a popular climbing school.

Serious watersports enthusiasts should consider a package deal through a specialist operator such as **Mark Warner**, one of several outfits that run sailing, windsurfing, water-skiing, kite-surfing and scuba-diving holidays in Corsica.

Objectif France offers bespoke self-drive tours of Corsica and other tailor-made experiences.

A dedicated cycling-holiday operator (among them, **Cycling-Corsica** or the UK-based **Hooked on Cycling**) can also arrange all your food and accommodation, as well as a support vehicle.

Wildlife enthusiasts should visit Corsica in the spring, when the maquis is in full flower, though knowing where and when to find the island's rarities does require specialist knowledge. UK-based **Nature Trek** is among the few dedicated operators in this field, and it offers an 8-day holiday based at various locations.

Any of the numerous diving schools operating in Corsica offer package deals that cover escorted dives, accommodation and meals in a single price. This tends to work out better value than making your own arrangements. Firms include **Corsica Diving Center** in Porticcio near Ajaccio and **Plongée Castille** in Calvi.

Dining

Corsica has an array of restaurants, ranging from high-end gastronomic temples in luxury hotels, to bars with snacks. By far the greatest concentration is in the coastal resorts (where nearly all close down from October to May) and in Ajaccio and Bastia. Most serve a mix of Corsican, French and Italian cuisine.

In rural areas, the choices are more limited; many restaurants are linked to hotels.

For a special treat, have a meal in a *ferme auberge*, where they serve traditional Corsican dishes based on home-grown produce. The **Gusti di Corsica** website has a complete list.

Most restaurants have a kids' menu priced at €10–18, offering smaller, more child-friendly meals. Restaurants in family-resort areas may even have highchairs.

As with everything else on the island, prices are on the high side. However most restaurants offer *menus fixe* (fixed-price menus), which invariably are better value for money than eating à la carte. You can also save money by ordering the house wine in carafes, or going for picnics: the island is dotted with beautiful spots for simple feasts of bread, cheese and charcuterie.

In general, tipping is optional. The *service*

compris on your bill or receipt means that a service charge has already been included, although a few extra coins are always appreciated by the staff.

If the bill says *service non compris* (or simply SNC), assume that a gratuity of about 10 per cent will be expected if you have received polite, prompt service in a restaurant.

Accommodation

Corsica has hotels to suit every pocket, ranging from inexpensive guest-houses in mountain villages, to chic boutique hotels on the coast, boasting designer decor and sleek infinity pools. The mid-range **Logis de France** association of hotels is also very well represented.

Self-catering holidays are the norm in Corsica, where the bulk of visitor accommodation is in rented villas, apartments and cottages. **Gîtes de France Corse**, the local branch of the country's largest self-catering group, has more than 1,350 rentals. The cost of a property is typically €900–2,850 per week, depending on the season. This may seem high, but it can be spread among two or three families.

Some of the best villas are block-booked by holiday companies; these often offer good flight-and-car-hire pack-age deals, especially for those who book early.

The French equivalent of "bed and breakfast", *chambres d'hôtes* are rooms attached to family homes. Warm hospitality is the norm. Rooms are nearly always en suite, and the breakfasts are enormous. Evening meals (*table d'hôte*) are sometimes also offered, especially in remote areas.

In a similar manner, *ferme-auberges* (farm inns) offer rooms with rustic character and fine Corsican cooking, often in spectacular locations. Listings are on the **Gusti di Corsica** and **Bienvenue à la Ferme** websites.

Corsica's long-distance hiking routes are all served by *gîtes d'étape* (for the coast-to-coast paths) and mountain refuges (on the GR20). The former offer bunks in four- to six-bed dorms; rates usually include obligatory half-board (*demi-pension*). Refuges are much more basic and may be booked via the Parc Naturel Régional de Corse's website (see p107).

Most Corsican campsites are equipped to the highest standards and are situated in great locations. They can get cramped in peak season but usually offer relaxing places to pitch a tent.

Because of the weight restrictions on economy flights, camping isn't a realistic option for most air travellers. Many camp-sites, however, offer tents, bungalows or mobile homes for rent.

Wherever you stay, reserve as far in advance as possible for peak season; nearly all hotels and holiday companies allow you to do this online through their websites. Sometimes, a deposit (*arrhes*) of 30 per cent has to be paid up front, although these days a cancellation fee may be deducted from your credit card if you fail to show up. Compare rates with offers on major websites such as **Booking.com**.

DIRECTORY

VISITOR INFORMATION

Corsica Isula
ⓦ corsica-isula.com

Visit Corsica
ⓦ visit-corsica.com

TRIPS AND TOURS

Corsica Aventure
ⓦ corsica-aventure.com

Corsica Diving Center
ⓦ corsicadivingcenter.com

Cycling-Corsica
ⓦ cycling-corsica.com

Hooked on Cycling
ⓦ hookedoncycling.co.uk

Keadventure
ⓦ keadventure.com

Mark Warner
ⓦ markwarner.co.uk

Nature Trek
ⓦ naturetrek.co.uk

Objectif France
ⓦ objectiffrance.com

Plongée Castille
ⓦ plongeecastille.com

Xtreme Sud
ⓦ xtremsud.com

ACCOMMODATION

Bienvenue à la Ferme
ⓦ bienvenue-a-la-ferme.com

Booking.com
ⓦ booking.com

Camping Corse
ⓦ campingcorse.com

Gîtes de France Corse
ⓦ gites-corsica.com

Gusti di Corsica
ⓦ gustidicorsica.com

Logis de France
ⓦ logishotels.com

Places to Stay

PRICE CATEGORIES
For a standard, double room per night (with breakfast if included), taxes and extra charges.

€ under €250   €€ €250–450   €€€ over €450

Luxury Hotels

U Palazzu Serenu
MAP E4 ■ Paganacce, Oletta ■ 04953 83939 ■ www.upalazzuserenu.com ■ €€
Corsica's only art hotel occupies a beautifully restored 17th-century mansion on the edge of Oletta village. Works by Anish Kapoor, Wendy Wischer and others adorn its nine rooms.

Casadelmar
MAP L5 ■ Route de Palombaggia, Porto-Vecchio ■ 04957 23434 ■ Closed Nov–mid-Apr ■ www.casadelmar.fr ■ €€€
A red-cedar and orange-granite exterior contrasts with the chic designer interiors of this boutique hotel that overlooks the Golfe de Porto-Vecchio. The water-side location, pool and spa are excellent, and the restaurant (see p89) is in a class of its own.

Domaine de Murtoli
MAP J5 ■ Vallee de l'Ortolo, Sartène ■ 04957 16924 ■ www.murtoli.com ■ €€€
This fabulously remote private estate is ranged above an inaccessible cove on the Sartenais coast. It comprises a scattering of old, luxuriously refurbished farmhouses, plus small swimming pools, a gastronomic restaurant and liveried staff.

Grand Hôtel de Cala Rossa
MAP L5 ■ Route de Cala Rossa, Lecci, Porto-Vecchio ■ 04957 16151 ■ Closed Nov–mid-Apr ■ www.hotel-calarossa.com ■ €€€
Driftwood furniture and teak decks are all part of the understated luxury at this exquisite hotel on the outskirts of Porto-Vecchio. It also boasts its own private beach, a beach-side bar, a spa and a fantastic Michelin-starred restaurant.

La Signoria
MAP B4 ■ Route de la Forêt de Bonifato, Calvi ■ 04956 59300 ■ Closed Dec–Mar ■ www.hotel-la-signoria.com ■ €€€
Festooned in citrus orchards and rose gardens, La Signoria is located about 4 km (3 miles) inland from Calvi, in a grand old farmhouse looking inland to the Balagne mountains. Oil paintings and distressed paintwork set the tone of the vintage-style interiors.

La Villa
MAP B4 ■ Chemin de Notre Dame de la Serra, Calvi ■ 04956 51010 ■ Closed mid-Oct–mid-Apr ■ www.hotel-lavilla.com ■ €€€
The real selling point of this five-star hotel is its superb view over Calvi's Citadelle and bay.

A sleek, modern place offering rooms, suites or separate villas, it boasts five pools, a spa and a Michelin-starred restaurant.

Le Hameau de Saparale
MAP K5 ■ 5 Cours Bonaparte, Sartène ■ 04957 17878 ■ Closed mid-Feb–mid-Mar ■ www.lehameaudesaparale.com ■ €€€
Set in the famed Domaine Saparale vineyards (see p69), these 19th-century guesthouses each have their own hammam and outdoor pool. Rates are comparable with those of a luxury hotel, but there is more space and privacy.

Miramar Boutique Hotel
MAP J5 ■ Route de la Corniche, Propriano ■ 04957 60613 ■ Closed mid-Oct–Apr ■ www.miramarboutiquehotel.com ■ €€€
This hotel has the feel of a secluded garden villa and enjoys a spectacular setting outside Propriano. All rooms have views over the Gulf of Valinco, as does the superb deck, with a heated pool and an excellent restaurant.

Seaside Hotels

La Solenzara
MAP L3 ■ Quartier du Palais, Solenzara ■ 04955 74218 ■ Open Apr–mid-Nov ■ www.lasolenzara.com ■ €
The flower-filled grounds of this stately 17th-century Genoese mansion overlook the beach. The rooms retain a period feel.

Pietracap

MAP F3 ▪ 20 Route de San Martino, Pietranera ▪ 04953 16463 ▪ Open Apr–Nov ▪ www.pietracap.com ▪ €
Located 3 km (2 miles) north of Bastia, this three-star hotel provides some rooms with balconies overlooking the Tyrrhenian Sea. There is also a pool and private access to a pebble beach.

La Roya

MAP E3 ▪ Plage de la Roya, St-Florent ▪ 04953 70040 ▪ Open mid-Mar–mid-Nov ▪ www.hotel delaroya.com ▪ €€
The rooms in this waterfront hotel near St-Florent are pleasantly furnished, the garden tumbles right down to the sand and the restaurant boasts a coveted Michelin star.

Le Goéland

MAP L5 ▪ La Marine, Ave Georges Pompidou, Porto-Vecchio ▪ 04957 01415 ▪ www.hotel goeland.com ▪ €€
This family-run hotel in Porto-Vecchio Marina is renowned for its elegance and simplicity. It has a prime beachfront location, and is just a brief walk from the Citadelle.

Le Lido

MAP J5 ▪ 42 Ave Napoléon, Propriano ▪ 04957 60637 ▪ Open end Apr–Sep ▪ www.le-lido.com ▪ €€
Positioned on a rocky promontory at the entrance to Propriano's harbour, Le Lido stands just above the water, surveying a gentle curve of white sand.

Le Pinarello

MAP L4 ▪ Plage de Pinarello, Sainte-Lucie-de-Porto-Vecchio ▪ 04957 14439 ▪ Open mid-Apr–mid-Oct ▪ www.lepinarello.com ▪ €€
Dominating the graceful arc of Pinarello beach, this hotel offers beautiful views from its stylish rooms, extending across the bay.

Les Bergeries de Palombaggia

MAP L6 ▪ Porto-Vecchio ▪ 04957 00323 ▪ Open mid-Apr–mid-Oct ▪ www.hotel-palombaggia.com ▪ €€
Granite and terracotta tiles dominate the exterior of this chic boutique hotel. The wood balconies, poolside deck, overflow pool and terraces offer a splendid view over one of the Mediterranean's loveliest beaches, bordered by umbrella pines.

U Capu Biancu

MAP K7 ▪ Route Canetto, Santa Manza, Bonifacio ▪ 04957 30558 ▪ Open May–mid-Oct ▪ www.ucapubiancu.com ▪ €€
A chic, secluded four-star hotel up the coast from Bonifacio, U Capu Biancu has idyllic bay views from its 39 rooms. The grounds, studded with granite boulders, feature a pool and adjoin two private beaches, one with an exclusive bar-restaurant.

Mountain Hotels

A Flatta

MAP C5 ▪ Calenzana ▪ 04956 28038 ▪ Open Apr–Oct ▪ www.aflatta.com ▪ €€
A boutique hotel hidden in the wild valley above Calenzana, A Flatta is especially well known for its gourmet restaurant. It also offers a handful of pool-facing rooms with contemporary four-poster beds, exposed beams and pretty gossamer drapes.

A Spelunca di u Sechju

MAP C4 ▪ Place de Village, Speloncato ▪ 04956 15038 ▪ Open Apr–Oct ▪ www.hotel-a-spelunca.com ▪ €
This charming village inn sits on the remains of an 11th-century fortress overlooking the Reginu Valley. The rooms are simple, but clean and comfortable. Excellent traditional cuisine is served on the terrace, with a view out to the mountains and the town square.

Casa Musicale

MAP C4 ▪ Place de l'Église, Pigna ▪ 04956 17731 ▪ Closed mid-Jan–Feb ▪ www.casa-musicale.org ▪ €
Wake up to the tinkling of sheeps' bells in this gem of a small hotel. Enjoy the views of the distant Balagne coast through windows framed by fig trees in delightful rooms painted in refreshing Mediterranean colours.

Chez Pierrot

MAP K4 ▪ Chez Pierrot, Hameau de Ghjallicu, Quenza, Alta Rocca ▪ 04957 86321 ▪ www.gitechezpierrot.free.fr ▪ €
This guesthouse is legendary for its rustic hospitality, homemade charcuterie and the post-prandial singalongs of the patron. Accommodation is in simple stone chalets, but the place offers superb value.

Hôtel de la Poste

MAP K4 ▪ Aullène ▪ 049 57 86121 ▪ Open May–Sep ▪ www.hotel-de-la-poste-aullene.com ▪ €

A 19th-century former coaching inn high in the hills of the Alta Rocca, De la Poste offers basic comforts (shared toilets only) but lots of old-world charm. The rates are good value.

Hôtel Dominique Colonna

MAP D6 ▪ Vallée de la Restonica, Corte ▪ 04954 52565 ▪ Open mid-Apr–Oct ▪ www.dominique-colonna.com ▪ €

Next to a mountain stream in the spectacular Vallée de la Restonica, this charming hotel is just the right place to relax, be it by the lovely pool during the day or by the open fire at night.

Hôtel Mare e Monti

MAP C4 ▪ Feliceto ▪ 04956 30200 ▪ Open mid-Apr–mid-Oct ▪ www.hotel-maremonti.com ▪ €

Dating from 1870, this hotel occupies an old palace, with a *belle époque* reception salon that has retained its original oil portraits and gilt tapestries. There's also a luxurious pool and a garden restaurant.

Palazzu Pigna

MAP C4 ▪ Pigna ▪ 04954 73278 ▪ Open Apr–Oct ▪ www.hotel-corse-palazzu.com ▪ €

This lovely heritage hotel occupies a sensitively restored early 18th-century manor house on a hilltop overlooking a glorious sweep of mountain and sea. The former seat of the Franceschini family, it is packed with heirlooms, and there is a superb terrace restaurant.

Town Hotels

Castel Brando

MAP F3 ▪ Erbalunga, Brando, Cap Corse ▪ 04953 01030 ▪ Open Apr–Oct ▪ www.castel brando.com ▪ €

The colour-washed walls, shuttered windows, schist roofs and palm-filled garden lend elegance to this 19th-century mansion. The vaulted interiors are filled with antiques, and there is an outdoor pool.

Centre Nautique

MAP K7 ▪ Quai Nord, Bonifacio ▪ 04957 30211 ▪ Open Apr–Oct ▪ www. centre-nautique.com ▪ €

Weary sailors alighting on the adjacent quayside form the mainstay of this waterfront boutique hotel, which, thanks to its location and gorgeous wood decor, rivals Le Genovese as the finest place to stay in Bonifacio.

Hôtel Kallisté

MAP P1 ▪ 51 Cours Napoléon, Ajaccio ▪ 04955 13445 ▪ www.hotel-kalliste-ajaccio.com ▪ €

This hotel fuses stylish modern furnishings with Napoleonic-era architecture to great effect. It enjoys a superb location in Ajaccio, with the cours Napoléon literally at its doorstep.

Hotel le Central

MAP N5 ▪ 3 Rue Miot, Bastia ▪ 04953 17112 ▪ www.centralhotel.fr ▪ €

Just off Bastia's place St-Nicolas, Le Central has smart and homely furnishings, friendly management and is brilliantly well maintained, ensuring it ranks among the best-value mid-range hotels on the island.

Hotel Santa Maria

MAP C4 ▪ Route du Port, L'Île Rousse ▪ 04956 30505 ▪ www.hotel santamaria.com ▪ €

The perfect place to stay in L'Île Rousse, Hotel Santa Maria has direct access to an adjacent beach. The rooms are comfortably furnished and some include sea-facing balconies.

Le Magnolia

MAP B4 ▪ Rue Alsace Lorraine, Calvi ▪ 04956 51916 ▪ Open Apr–Oct ▪ www.hotel-le-magnolia.com ▪ €

This *belle époque*-style hotel is housed in a 19th-century residence just behind Calvi's Quai Landry. Le Magnolia derives its name from the 100-year-old tree in its courtyard.

Les Voyageurs

MAP N4 ▪ 9 Ave Maréchal Sebastiani, Bastia ▪ 04953 49080 ▪ www.hotel-les voyageurs-bastia.com ▪ €

With quirkily themed rooms ("Indians", "Jules Verne", "Cinema" and the like), this family-run hotel in Bastia possesses an idiosyncratic charm. It offers three-star comforts at very reasonable prices.

San Damianu

MAP J5 ▪ Quartier San Damien, Sartène ▪ 04957 05541 ▪ Open Apr–Oct ▪ www.sandamianu.fr ▪ €

A smart Best Western hotel on a natural balcony, which overlooks Sartène's medieval roofscape and

Rizzanese valley, San Damianu is one of the top places to stay in town. Rooms boast their own private terraces.

Les Mouettes

MAP N3 ■ 9 Cours Lucien Bonaparte, Ajaccio ■ 04955 04040 ■ Open Mar–Oct ■ www.hotel lesmouettes.fr ■ €€

A luxurious hotel, Les Mouettes dates from Ajaccio's 19th-century heyday and is in a splendid location on the route des Sanguinaires, looking straight across the gulf. It offers all the swank and modern conveniences that you would expect from a four-star hotel.

Hôtel Genovese

MAP K7 ■ Haute Ville, Place de l'Europe, Bonifacio ■ 04957 31234 ■ Open Jan–Nov ■ www. hotel-genovese.com ■ €€€

This five-star hotel overlooks Bonifacio's port from a ledge beside the Citadelle walls. The earthy interiors open on to a secluded courtyard, with a pool, lit up by candles and lanterns at night.

Bed & Breakfasts

Casa Capellini

MAP E6 ■ Sant'Andrea di Bozio, Bozio, near Corte ■ 06147 44498 ■ Open Apr–Oct ■ www. chambres-hotes-corse-boziu.com ■ €

A 1930s grocer's shop has been converted into a guesthouse of great charm. While the meals prepared from local organic produce get rave reviews the real highlight of this B&B is its valley views.

Casa Maria

MAP E3 ■ Nonza, Cap Corse ■ 04953 78095 ■ www.casamaria-corse. com ■ €

Located just off Nonza's square, Casa Maria's impeccably clean, tiled rooms look out from the gulf of St-Florent to the coast of the Désert des Agriate. Breakfast is served on a lovely sun-dappled terrace.

Château Cagninacci

MAP E3 ■ San Martino di Lota, near Bastia ■ 06782 90394 ■ Open mid-May–Sep ■ www.chateau cagninacci.com ■ €

This aristocratic B&B, in a little-visited corner of Cap Corse, occupies an old Capuchin convent – a rambling, mid-17th-century pile set around a central cloister. Rooms are spacious and well equipped, and the hosts are friendly and helpful.

Chez Antoinette et Charles

MAP D7 ■ Saint Pierre de Venaco ■ 04954 70729, 06039 26083 ■ Open Apr–mid-Oct ■ antoinette.charles. free.fr ■ €

Set in a grand old Venachais house, this B&B doubles as a lodge for hikers. A lively, convivial atmosphere prevails on its terrace in summer. All four rooms on offer are en suite and very pleasantly furnished.

Chez Gilles et Elise

MAP E3 ■ Figarella and Miomo, Cap Corse ■ 04953 32565 ■ www. medori.net ■ €

The sunny terrace of this pretty schist cottage looks down the valley

and out to sea. The rooms, despite being small, are tastefully furnished, and the breakfasts are huge.

La Diligence

MAP E6 ■ Verdèse, near Campana, Castagniccia ■ 04953 42633 ■ Closed for a few wks between mid-Dec & mid-Jan ■ www.la-diligence. net ■ €

A homely, inexpensive B&B on the edge of one of Castagniccia's prettiest and most remote villages, La Diligence offers beautifully decorated rooms and sweeping views from its terrace over the chestnut canopy. The hosts are also able to rustle up some delicious local cuisine.

L'Altu Pratu

MAP E7 ■ Erbajola, Bozio, near Corte ■ 04954 88007 ■ Open Apr–Oct ■ www. altupratu.com ■ €

On the outskirts of Bozio village, this modern house offers spacious, en-suite rooms. There's a fair-sized pool and, after dinner, the host regales guests with Corsican songs accompanied by a mandolin and guitar.

Littariccia

MAP L6 ■ Route de Palombaggia, near Porto-Vecchio ■ 04957 04133 ■ Open Mar–Dec (some rooms available in Jan & Feb) ■ www.littariccia. com ■ €

Set amid a grove of olive trees on a hillside overlooking the plage de Palombaggia, Littariccia is more like a boutique hotel, with orange-granite architecture and artfully styled, sea-facing rooms.

For a key to hotel price categories see p112

U Chyosu di a Petra
MAP C4 ■ Olmi Capella, Giunssani ■ 04956 19101 ■ www.locations-corses. com ■ €
Perched on the flank of a mountainside in the isolated Giunssani region this B&B is set in a fairly remote location. The building looks as old as the hills but it was actually built relatively recently using reclaimed materials.

Domaine de Croccano
MAP J5 ■ Route de Granace, near Sartène ■ 04957 71137 ■ Closed Dec–Jan ■ www.corse nature.com ■ €€
This superb 18th-century farmhouse has everything you could wish for from a Corsican B&B: views across rolling maquis and vineyards to the sea, fine dining, guided walks, horseback promenades and warm hospitality.

Campsites

Arepos Roccapina
MAP J6 ■ Baie de Roccapina, Sartenais ■ 04957 71930 ■ Open May–Sep ■ €
Brave the bone-jarring, 2.5-km (1.5-mile) drive down a rough track from the nearest main road, and the rewards are an inexpensive campsite behind an exquisite bay of powder-white sand and turquoise water. Watch out for mosquitoes in summertime.

Camping d'Arone
MAP A7 ■ Plage d'Arone, Piana ■ 04952 06454 ■ Open mid-May–Sep ■ €
This slick, professionally run site is located a short walk away from a glorious beach of golden sand and blue water, and it is flanked by wild hillsides. Although busy in high season, at other times it is a quiet and secluded spot to stay in for a week or more.

Camping Monte-Cinto
MAP C6 ■ Lozzi, Vallée de Niolo ■ 04954 78608 ■ Open May–Oct ■ www. campingmontecinto-asco.com ■ €
You can almost reach out and touch Corsica's highest peak from the leafy terraces of this remote campsite in a chestnut grove on the elevated northern flank of the Vallée de Niolo.

Camping Tuani
MAP D7 ■ Vallée de la Restonica ■ 04954 61165/61962 ■ Open mid-Apr–mid-Sep ■ www.camping-corte.com ■ €
For the full-on Restonica experience, camp under the 100-year-old pines beside a rushing mountain torrent where you can swim in deep, green pools. Close to the trail for Monte Rotondo, Camping Tuani makes the perfect base from which to embark on walking adventures.

L'Albadu
MAP D6 ■ Centre Equestre Albadu Pulicani, Ancienne Route d'Ajaccio, Corte ■ 04954 62455 ■ €
This rustic farm, at a horse-riding centre on the hillside over Corte, has terrific views and first-rate facilities, including a restaurant. There is always plenty of room, but it is a bit of a trek from the town centre by public transport.

La Vetta
MAP L5 ■ Trinité de Porto-Vecchio, RN 198, Porto-Vecchio ■ 04957 00986 ■ Open Jun–Sep ■ www.campinglavetta. com ■ €
Enjoy a peaceful woodsy setting near Porto-Vecchio at this family-oriented four-star campsite. There are adult and children's pools, and a choice of mobile homes and chalets. The bar-restaurant (open Jul & Aug) has free Wi-Fi.

Le Bodri
MAP C4 ■ RN 197, Route de Calvi, Corbara ■ 04956 01086 ■ Open May–Sep ■ www.campinglebodri. com ■ €
A sprawling campsite, Le Bodri gets incredibly crowded in high summer but is virtually empty in shoulder season. It is right above a pair of divine little beaches with pure-white sand.

Plage U Stazzu
MAP F1 ■ Route Acqua Salse, 1 km (0.5 mile) north of Macinaggio, Cap Corse ■ 04953 54376 ■ Open mid-May–Sep ■ www.camping-u-stazzu.jimdo.com ■ €
The rock-hard, sloping ground at this small site at the tip of Cap Corse will take its toll on your tent pegs, but it is close to town and a 5-minute walk from the beach. It also runs a popular pizzeria.

Sole e Vista
MAP B6 ■ Centre ville, Porto ■ 04952 61571 ■ Open Apr–Oct ■ www. camping-sole-e-vista.fr ■ €
The most atmospheric of four large campsites in the Spelunca Gorge

on the west coast, Sole e Vista's varied forest cover and irregular terracing retains the feel of a wild camp – though it has well-maintained sanitary blocks and a café.

Gîtes d'Étapes

A Funtana

MAP B6 ■ 12, Hameau Montestremo, Manso, Vallée du Fango ■ 06154 38454 ■ Open Apr–Oct ■ http://gite-afuntana. jimdo.com ■ €

Montestremo is the most remote location reachable by surfaced road in Corsica. The village gîte serves as a comfortable base for forays into the nearby wilderness.

Auberge du Col de Bavella

MAP L4 ■ Col de Bavella, Zonza ■ 04957 20987, 06131 41733 ■ Open Apr–Nov ■ www.auberge-bavella.com ■ €

This superb lodge on the roadside below the Col de Bavella faces the famous Aiguilles de Bavella. Its wood-lined interior is filled with hiking, climbing and hunting memorabilia. The hostel has its own self-catering kitchen, and there is also a cosy restaurant on-site.

Bella Vista

MAP K3 ■ Cozzano, Haut Taravo ■ 04952 44159 ■ Open Apr–mid-Oct ■ www.gitecozzano hebergementcorse. com ■ €

There are sunny, six-bed dorms with panoramic views over the Haut Taravo valley at this gîte. Host Baptiste Pantalacci brings a great sense of vocation to his role as warden, and

the meals his mother prepares, using his father's own free-range charcuterie, are excellent.

E Case

MAP G1 ■ Parc Naturel Regional de Corse, Revinda, near Cargèse ■ 04952 64819 ■ Open Apr–Sep ■ €

Run by the National Park Authority and half an hour's trek from Revinda, E Case occupies an old shepherd's hut where you can eat hearty mountain cooking and admire the gorgeous Mediterranean landscape from an ancient stone terrace.

Gîte L'Alivi

MAP B6 ■ Serriera ■ 04951 04933 ■ Open Apr–Oct ■ €

Set in an old olive oil mill, L'Alivi is a quaint refuge for hikers and vacationers. The basic dorm-style rooms are simple and rustic. The delicious local cuisine is more than sufficient to prepare you for a day in the stunning Corsica National Park.

Gîte L'Alzelli

MAP B5 ■ Galeria, Tuarelli ■ 04956 20175, 06204 84986 ■ Open Mid-Apr–mid-Oct ■ €

This lodge features on the penultimate day of the Tra Mare e Monti Nord route along the west coast. Set in the middle of the mountains, next to a splendid river, it is a superb place to end a day's hiking.

La Cabane du Berger

MAP B6 ■ Girolata, Osani ■ 04952 01698 ■ Open Apr–Oct ■ €

There are two separate gîtes in Girolata. This one is the nicer of the two,

with pleasant little wood cabins under the eucalyptus trees behind the beach and a waterfront café.

U Cartalavonu

MAP K5 ■ Ospédale, Porto-Vecchio ■ 04957 00039 ■ Open Apr–Oct ■ www.lerefuge-cartalavonu.com ■ €

With its maritime pine forest and ghoulish boulder outcrops, the Massif de l'Ospédale (see p87) rising inland from Porto-Vecchio has its own distinct atmosphere. This well-run little gîte, located on the Mare a Mare Sud route, oozes local character and has an open fire and lively bar.

U Poghju

MAP B7 ■ Capo Sottano, Evisa ■ 04952 62188, 06324 23041 ■ Open Apr–Oct ■ www.gite-detape-evisa.com ■ €

This lodge has long enjoyed a strong reputation among Tra Mare e Monti Nord hikers for its spacious dorms, warm hospitality and generous wood-grilled suppers, served alfresco on the terrace or in the shaded garden.

Ustaria di a Rota

MAP B7 ■ Marignana ■ 04952 62121 ■ www. ustariadiarota.fr ■ €

Host Paul Ceccaldi's famous hospitality, which extends from excellent food to after-dinner songs, explains the near-legendary status of this gîte-cum-refuge, high in the hinterland of Porto on the Mare a Mare Nord/Tra Mare e Monti trails.

For a key to hotel price categories see p112

Index

Acknowledgments

Author
Richard Abram

Additional contributor
Dana Facaros

Publishing Director Georgina Dee

Publisher Vivien Antwi

Design Director Phil Ormerod

Editorial Sophie Adam, Michelle Crane, Rachel Fox, Priyanka Kumar, Alison McGill, Sally Schafer, Sands Publishing Solutions

Cover Design Bess Daly, Maxine Pedliham

Design Tessa Bindloss, Bharti Karakoti

Picture Research Sumita Khatwani, Ellen Root, Lucy Sienkowska

Cartography Stuart James, Jasneet Kaur, Zafar-ul-Islam Khan, Suresh Kumar, James Macdonald, Casper Morris

DTP Jason Little

Production Olivia Jeffries

Factchecker Michelle Arness Frederic

Proofreader Ruth Reisenberger

Indexer Helen Peters

Revisions Hansa Babra, Dipika Dasgupta, Shikha Kulkarni, Kanika Praharaj, Azeem Siddiqui, Tanveer Zaidi

Commissioned Photography Rough Guides/David Abram, Tony Souter

Picture Credits

The publisher would like to thank the following for their kind permission to reproduce their photographs:

Key: a-above; b-below/bottom; c-centre; f-far; l-left; r-right; t-top

123RF.com: freeartist 1; Ran Dembo 95tl.

A Cupulatta: 62c.

A Pignata: 66br.

Alamy Stock Photo: age fotostock/J.D. Dallet 98tl, 100br; AU Photos 57tr; blickwinkel/Royal 46clb; Christophe Boisvieux 54b, 73cl; Jerome Cornier 50cr; Janos Csernoch 94–5, 96tl; Ian Dagnall 30cl; Danita Delimont/Walter Bibikow 13bc, 101cl; Detail Nottingham 64cla; EDB Image Archive 72bl; freeartist 28–9; guichaoua 20r; Chris Hellier 26clb; hemis.fr/Georges Antoni 17tl, /Stéphane Frances 16–17, /Camille Moirenc 68cr, /Bertrand Rieger 42tl, 69tr, 88tl; imageBROKER /Peter Giovannini 100t, /Martina Katz 70bl, /Martin Moxter 12crb, /Kevin Prönnecke 80tr, /Konrad Wothe 79cla; jaileybug 56cl; Art Kowalsky 2tl, 8–9; LatitudeStock /David Forman 67tr; Jonathan Little 65br; Martin Thomas Photography 71tl; Eric Nathan 63clb; Nature Picture Library/Angelo Gandolfi 11tr, 100clb; Kasia Nowak 94cl; Frederic Pacorel 53tr; Photocuisine/Ginet-Drin 71br; Dirk Renckhoff 35crb; Raphael Salzedo 73tr; Antony Souter 21tl, 47tr, 69b; StockShot/John Wilhelmsson 55tl; Travelshots.com/Peter Phipp 10cra; Jan Wlodarczyk 4cr, 6br, 10cr, 10crb, 11tl, 26–7, 30–31, 34–5, 50b; Zoonar GmbH 30bl; Didier Zylberyng 29br.

AWL Images: Walter Bibikow 3tl, 3tr, 4clb, 7tl, 13tr, 48bl, 74–5, 104–5b; Hemis 2tr, 4b, 36–7, 52br, 54cr.

Bonifacio Tourism: 4t, 21cl, 21crb.

Casa Musicale: 103bl.

Corbis: Axiom Photographic 82cl; Dr. Wilfried Bahnmüller 40cla; Marc Dozier 22cl, 32–3, 39bl, 43tr; Hemis/Rene Mattes 34cla; Lebrecht Music & Arts 38cr; Jean-Pierre Lescourret 24–5.

Corsica Madness: 63tr.

Le DIAN'ARTE Museum: 23tc.

Dreamstime.com: Allard 93tl; Allard1 18br; Per Björkdahl 31clb; Steven Blandin 59clb; Csimages 52tl; Edwardstaines 85tr; Eugenesergeev 6cla, 18–19, 55br, 76l, 78t, 79bl, 85bl; Jiri Foltyn 34clb; Honzahruby 84ca; Jon Ingall 60cl, 80b, 102t; Joningall 56t, 93crb; Margouillat 65cl; Micca44 49b; Mikelane45 58cra; Morseicinque 58bc; Naturefriend 42crb; Odrachenko 11clb, 35bl; Sabino Parente 65tl; Photogolfer 77cr; Photoprofi30 86b; Juan Ignacio Polo 81cr; Rndmst 22–3, 23br, 27tl, 27crb, 32bl, 41clb, 43cl, 79tl; Salajean 78clb; Volodymyr Shevchuk 59tl; Bidouze Stéphane 59br; Tatouata 44clb; Ventura69 47b; Xdrew 40b; Dušan Zidar 51cr, 99b; Rudmer Zwerver 58clb.

Getty Images: AFP/Pascal Pochard 51tl, 71clb; hemis.fr/Franck Guiziou 19br; LEGRAND 70t; Three Lions/Evans 39cla; Leslie West 12–13.

iStockphoto.com: dulezidar 12cl; gege2812 31cr; hardyuno 87cl; Wiktory 64br.

Martin Lendi: 16bl, 28clb, 41br.

Les Nuits de la Guitare: Frédéric Dupertuys 72t.

Palais Fesch, Musée des Beaux Arts: 15bl; RMN/Gérard Blot 14tl, 15cra.

Le Pirate: 66t.

Robert Harding Picture Library: Walter

Bibikow 33clb, 86cla; Nelly Boyd 62tr; J.D. Dallet 4crb; Ken Gillham 38bc; Gavin Hellier 4cl; Markus Lange 44t; Ellen Rooney 48t; Yadid Levy 32cl.

SuperStock: age fotostock/Eric Farrelly 77tl; DeAgostini 38cla; Hemis.fr 53cl; imageBROKER 57bl, 61cr; Jim Kahnweiler 90–91; LOOK-foto 11cr; Photononstop 61tl; Kevin Prönnecke/imageBROKER 45bl.

Le Tamaricciu: 89cl.

Cover

Front and spine: **Alamy Stock Photo:** Eva Bocek.

Back: **Alamy Stock Photo:** Eva Bocek bc; **AWL Images:** Doug Pearson cla; **Dreamstime.com:** Hornet83 tl; **iStockphoto. com:** pkazmierczak tr; **Robert Harding Picture Library:** Stuart Black crb.

Pull Out Map Cover
Alamy Stock Photo: Eva Bocek.

All other images © Dorling Kindersley
For further information see:
www.dkimages.com

*As a guide to abbreviations in visitor information blocks: **Adm** = admission charge; **D** = Dinner; **L** = Lunch.*

Penguin
Random
House

Printed and bound in China

First edition 2012

Published in Great Britain by
Dorling Kindersley Limited
80 Strand, London WC2R 0RL

Published in the United States by
DK Publishing, 345 Hudson Street,
New York, New York 10014

Copyright © 2012, 2019 Dorling
Kindersley Limited

A Penguin Random House Company

18 19 20 21 10 9 8 7 6 5 4 3 2 1

Reprinted with revisions 2014, 2017, 2019

ISSN 1479-344X

ISBN 978-0-2413-6465-9

SPECIAL EDITIONS OF DK TRAVEL GUIDES

DK Travel Guides can be purchased
in bulk quantities at discounted prices
for use in promotions or as premiums.
We also offer special editions and
personalized jackets, corporate
imprints, and excerpts from all
our books, tailored specifically
to meet your needs.

To find out more, please contact:

in the US
specialsales@dk.com
in the UK
travelguides@uk.dk.com
in Canada
specialmarkets@dk.com
in Australia
**penguincorporatesales@
penguinrandomhouse.com.au**

Phrase Book

In Emergency

Help!	Au secours!	oh sekoor
Stop!	Arrêtez!	aret-ay
Call a doctor!	Appelez un médecin!	apuh-lay uñ medsañ
Call an ambulance!	Appelez une ambulance!	apuh-lay oon oñboo-loñs
Call the police!	Appelez la police!	apuh-lay lah poh-lees
Call the fire brigade!	Appelez les pompiers!	apuh-lay leh poñ-peeyay

Communication Essentials

Yes/No	Oui/Non	wee/noñ
Please	S'il vous plaît	seel voo play
Thank you	Merci	mer-see
Excuse me	Excusez-moi	exkoo-zay mwah
Hello	Bonjour	boñzhoor
Goodbye	Au revoir	oh ruh-vwar
Good night	Bonsoir	boñ-swar
What?	Quel, quelle?	kel, kel
When?	Quand?	koñ
Why?	Pourquoi?	poor-kwah
Where?	Où?	oo

Useful Phrases

How are you?	Comment allez-vous?	kom-moñ talay voo
Very well,	Très bien	treh byañ
Pleased to meet you.	Enchanté de faire votre connaissance.	oñshoñ-tay duh fehr votr kon-ay-sans
Where is/are…?	Où est/sont…?	oo ay/soñ
Which way to…?	Quelle est la direction pour?	kel ay lah deer-ek-syoñ poor
Do you speak English?	Parlez-vous anglais?	par-lay voo oñg-lay
I don't understand.	Je ne comprends pas.	zhuh nuh kom-proñ pah.
I'm sorry.	Excusez-moi.	exkoo-zay mwah

Useful Words

big	grand	groñ
small	petit	puh-tee
hot	chaud	show
cold	froid	frwah
good	bon	boñ
bad	mauvais	moh-veh
open	ouvert	oo-ver
closed	fermé	fer-meh
left	gauche	gohsh
right	droit	drwah
entrance	l'entrée	l'on-tray
exit	la sortie	sor-tee

Shopping

How much does this cost?	C'est combien s'il vous plaît?	say kom-byañ seel voo play
I would like…	Je voudrais…	zhuh voo-dray
Do you have?	Est-ce que vous avez?	es-kuh voo zavay
Do you take credit cards?	Est-ce que vous acceptez les cartes de crédit?	es-kuh voo zaksept-ay leh kart duh kreh-dee
What time do you open?	A quelle heure vous êtes ouvert?	ah kel urr voo zet oo-ver
What time do you close?	A quelle heure vous êtes fermé?	ah kel urr voo zet fer-may
This one.	Celui-ci.	suhl-wee-see
That one.	Celui-là.	suhl-wee-lah
expensive	cher	shehr
cheap	pas cher, bon marché	pah shehr, boñ mar-shay
size, clothes	la taille	tye
size, shoes	la pointure	pwañ-tur
white	blanc	bloñ
black	noir	nwahr
red	rouge	roozh
yellow	jaune	zhohwn
green	vert	vehr
blue	bleu	bluh

Types of Shop

antique shop	le magasin d'antiquités	maga-zañ d'oñteekee-tay
bakery	la boulangerie	booloñ-zhuree
bank	la banque	boñk
bookshop	la librairie	lee-brehree
cake shop	la pâtisserie	patee-sree
cheese shop	la fromagerie	fromazh-ree
chemist	la pharmacie	farmah-see
department store	le grand magasin	groñ maga-zañ
delicatessen	la charcuterie	sharkoot-ree
gift shop	le magasin de cadeaux	maga-zañ duh kadoh
greengrocer	le marchand de légumes	mar-shoñ duh lay-goom
grocery	l'alimentation	alee-moñta-syoñ
market	le marché	marsh-ay
newsagent	le magasin de journaux	maga-zañ duh zhoor-no
post office	la poste, le bureau de poste, le PTT	pohst, booroh duh pohst, peh-teh-teh
supermarket	le supermarché	soo pehr-marshay
tobacconist	le tabac	tabah
travel agent	l'agence de voyages	l'azhoñs duh vwayazh

Sightseeing

abbey	l'abbaye	l'abay-ee
art gallery	la galerie d'art	galer-ree dart
bus station	la gare routière	gahr roo-tee-yehr
cathedral	la cathédrale	katay-dral
church	l'église	l'aygleez
garden	le jardin	zhar-dañ
library	la bibliothèque	beebleeo-tek
museum	le musée	moo-zay
railway station	la gare (SNCF)	gahr (es-en-say-ef)
tourist information office	renseignements touristiques, le, syndicat d'initiative	roñsayn-moñ toorees-teek sandee-ka d'eenee-syateev
town hall	l'hôtel de ville	l'ohtel duh veel

Staying in a Hotel

Do you have a vacant room?	Est-ce que vous avez une chambre?	es-kuh voo-zavay oon shambr
double room, with double bed	la chambre à deux personnes, avec un grand lit	shambrah duh pehr-son avek un groñ lee

twin room	la chambre à deux lits	shambr ah duh lee
single room	la chambre à une personne	shambr ah oon pehr-son
room with a bath, shower	la chambre avec salle de bains, une douche	shambr avek sal duh bañ, oon doosh
I have a reservation.	J'ai fait une réservation.	zhay fay oon rayzehrva-syoñ

Eating Out

Have you got a table?	Avez-vous une table de libre?	avay-voo oon tahbl duh leebr
I want to reserve a table.	Je voudrais réserver une table.	zhuh voo-dray rayzehr-vay on tahbl
The bill please.	L'addition s'il vous plaît.	'ladee-syoñ seel voo play
Waitress/ waiter	Madame, Mademoiselle/ Monsieur	mah-dam, mah-demwahzel/ muh-syuh
menu	le menu, la carte	men-oo, kart
fixed-price menu	le menu à prix fixe	men-oo ah pree feeks
cover charge	le couvert	koo-vehr
wine list	la carte des vins	kart-deh vañ
glass	le verre	vehr
bottle	la bouteille	boo-tay
knife	le couteau	koo-toh
fork	la fourchette	for-shet
spoon	la cuillère	kwee-yehr
breakfast	le petit déjeuner	puh-tee deh-zhuh-nay
lunch	le déjeuner	deh-zhuh-nay
dinner	le dîner	dee-nay
main course	le plat principal	plah prañsee-pal
starter, first course	l'entrée, le hors d'oeuvre	'oñ-tray, or-duhvr
dish of the day	le plat du jour	plah doo zhoor
wine bar	le bar à vin	bar ah vañ
café	le café	ka-fay

Menu Decoder

baked	cuit au four	kweet oh foor
beef	le boeuf	buhf
beer	la bière	bee-yehr
boiled	bouilli	boo-yee
bread	le pain	pan
butter	le beurre	burr
cake	le gâteau	gah-toh
cheese	le fromage	from-azh
chicken	le poulet	poo-lay
chips	les frites	freet
chocolate	le chocolat	shoko-lah
coffee	le café	kah-fay
dessert	le dessert	deh-ser
egg	l'oeuf	'uf
fish	le poisson	pwah-ssoñ
fresh fruit	le fruit frais	frwee freh
garlic	l'ail	'eye
grilled	grillé	gree-yay
ham	le jambon	zhoñ-boñ
ice, ice cream	la glace	glas
lamb	l'agneau	'anyoh
lemon	le citron	see-troñ
meat	la viande	vee-yand
milk	le lait	leh
mineral water	l'eau minérale	'oh meeney-ral
oil	l'huile	'weel
onions	les oignons	leh zonyoñ

fresh orange juice	l'orange pressée	l'oroñzh press-eh
fresh lemon juice	le citron pressé	see-troñ press-eh
pepper	le poivre	pwavr
pork	le porc	por
potatoes	pommes de terre	pom-duh tehr
rice	le riz	ree
roast	rôti	row-tee
salt	le sel	sel
sausage, fresh	la saucisse	sohsees
seafood	les fruits de mer	frwee duh mer
snails	les escargots	leh zes-kar-goh
soup	la soupe, le potage	soop, poh-tazh
steak	le bifteck	beef-tek, stek
sugar	le sucre	sookr
tea	le thé	tay
vegetables	les légumes	lay-goom
vinegar	le vinaigre	veenaygr
water	l'eau	'oh
red wine	le vin rouge	vañ roozh
white wine	le vin blanc	vañ bloñ

Numbers

0	zéro	zeh-roh
1	un, une	uñ, oon
2	deux	duh
3	trois	trwah
4	quatre	katr
5	cinq	sañk
6	six	sees
7	sept	set
8	huit	weet
9	neuf	nerf
10	dix	dees
11	onze	oñz
12	douze	dooz
13	treize	trehz
14	quatorze	katorz
15	quinze	kañz
16	seize	sehz
17	dix-sept	dees-set
18	dix-huit	dees-weet
19	dix-neuf	dees-nerf
20	vingt	vañ
30	trente	tront
40	quarante	karoñt
50	cinquante	sañkoñt
60	soixante	swasoñt
70	soixante-dix	swasoñt-dees
80	quatre-vingts	katr-vañ
90	quatre-vingt-dix	katr-vañ-dees
100	cent	soñ
1,000	mille	meel

Time

one minute	une minute	oon mee-noot
one hour	une heure	oon urr
half an hour	une demi-heure	urr duh-me urr
one day	un jour	urr zhorr
Monday	lundi	luñ-dee
Tuesday	mardi	mar-dee
Wednesday	mercredi	mehrkruh-dee
Thursday	jeudi	zhuh-dee
Friday	vendredi	voñdruh-dee
Saturday	samedi	sam-dee
Sunday	dimanche	dee-moñsh

Selected Corsica Index